The Interview Kit

THE INTERVIEW KIT

RICHARD H. BEATTY

JOHN WILEY & SONS, INC.

New York • Chichester • Brisbane • Toronto • Singapore

Library of Congress Cataloging-in-Publication Data:

Beatty, Richard H.
      The interview kit / by Richard H. Beatty.
          p.   cm.
      Includes bibliographical references.
      ISBN 0-471-12404-4 (pbk. alk. paper)
      1. Employment interviewing.   I. Title.
    HF5549.5.I68387   1995
    650.14—dc20 95-34905

Printed in the United States of America

10 9 8 7 6 5 4

To my black cock-a-poo, Muffin, who lovingly lay at my feet while I wrote this book at our beach house.

And to my loving, outgoing, talkative wife, Carolyn, who exercised enormous restraint in tiptoeing around me while patiently waiting for me to finish.

PREFACE

I believe that you will find this to be the most comprehensive and practical book on interviewing on the market today. It is loaded with practical, usable information that I feel you will find very helpful in preparing for an employment interview—whether you are a first-time, novice job seeker or a skilled, seasoned professional. There is sure to be something for everyone, from college senior to chief executive officer.

Highlights of the book include strategies for answering over 500 commonly-asked interview questions covering a wide range of candidate selection-related topics. These are those tough questions that the employer will use to separate the top candidates from the "also rans." Having the right answers to these questions will substantially enhance your probability of getting the job offer. Much of this book is committed to helping you develop those "right" answers.

If you can answer these key questions, I believe you will be prepared to handle almost anything the employer will throw at you—with ease!

Another key feature is Chapter 4 on "Damage Control in the Interview." This chapter is crammed full of helpful tricks and techniques for effectively avoiding the traps and pitfalls of the interview. What do you do when the employer goes after some of your weaknesses—the areas you know need improvement, what you don't like about your boss, etc. Candidates fail interviews when they don't know how to handle these questions. This book helps you chart a safe course through these rough interview waters, and keeps your candidacy afloat.

I think you will find Chapter 3, "Five Winning Interview Strategies," particularly enlightening in understanding what it takes to succeed in the interview and get the offer. Detailed here are 5 real-life interview strategies used by thousands of employment candidates to distinguish them from the pack and gain a real advantage over competition. You won't just get the theory, but also the practical advice of how to use these strategies to your own advantage.

Chapter 23, "Closing the Interview," is unique when compared to other books on interviewing. This chapter instructs you on exactly how to close the employment interview to your advantage. It shows you how to get valuable feedback on the interview, and what to do with it. It will teach you how to use these last few closing moments in the interview discussion to enhance the employer's interest in your candidacy, and how to be sure you have common agreement on what the next steps will be.

I think you will find the general approach to this book extremely helpful. The chapters are laid out (as with most of my employment books) in such a way as to present a logical, step-by-step approach to the entire interview process—moving from advance preparation for the interview, to the interview itself, to how to handle yourself as you depart. The book is loaded with specific advice and lots of practical examples.

Whether you are the beginning interviewee or the heavily seasoned executive who has considerable interviewing experience, I think you will find this book an excellent aid to preparing you for a successful employment interview.

Good luck in your interviews!

RICHARD H. BEATTY

West Chester, Pennsylvania
August 1995

CONTENTS

1

BEFORE THE INTERVIEW

I t has always been surprising how many people go off to an employment interview hoping to get a job offer and yet have done little or nothing to actually prepare for the interview. Having been an employment manager for a major corporation, I have observed time and time again those who show up for the interview who have little or no advance knowledge about either the company or the job for which they are about to interview. Less than 20 percent of the candidates I have interviewed over the years have done any preliminary research into the company with which they are considering spending a good portion of their career.

This is unfortunate when we think about the importance of having the right job with the right company. Our job affects so many important parts of our lives that it is hard to imagine why most employment candidates devote so little time to researching this important decision.

The importance of good job selection is self-evident. Jobs that are interesting, challenging, and stimulating can add much to the quality of our lives. Since most people spend more of their waking hours engaged in work than any other activity, enjoying what we are doing for a living is important to our sense of happiness and self-fulfillment. In this age of corporate downsizing and leaner organizations, most people are finding that they must devote an ever-increasing portion of their time engaged in work-related activities.

Our work has a lot to do with our self-image. Much of how we feel about ourselves is connected with our work. If we enjoy our work and are good at what we are doing, we feel a sense of pride, achievement, energy, and inner fulfillment. Life is good!

On the other hand, when we find our work uninteresting, difficult, or unrewarding, these positive feelings are crowded out and give way to feelings of doubt, insecurity, lack of self-confidence, loss of pride, and a sense of general depression. Life is miserable, and so are we!

How we feel about our job also has a way of spilling over into our personal lives, affecting not only ourselves but those around us. The old adage of the disgruntled worker who goes home and kicks the dog may have more truth than fiction. The continuous stress of an unrewarding job or work environment cannot only cause depression, but can also generate feelings of insensitivity, defensiveness, and general hostility. Sooner or later these negative feelings affect our relationships with those for whom we care the most.

The good news is that we can change all of that if we really want to. Fortunately we live in a country that affords us the freedom and guarantees us the inalienable right to pursue happiness. Job change can often be the vehicle to pursue such happiness and good interviewing skills are the tools for realizing it.

ADVANCE RESEARCH

The goal of effective interviewing is really twofold: One is to get the job offer and the other is land a stimulating, rewarding job in a company where you enjoy working. In my judgment (and hopefully yours), both of these goals are too important to simply leave them to chance.

There's an old saying, "Chance favors the prepared mind." Nothing could be more true than this in the case of the employment interview. Landing a good job is not nearly so much a matter of luck as it is a matter of good planning and advance preparation. I suggest you devote some serious effort to researching and preparing for the job interview.

As will become readily apparent to you later in this book, having advance knowledge of the company and its culture (i.e., work environment) is vital to preparing a winning interview strategy. There are many interview questions that are aimed at determining whether or not you will blend in well with the work environment of the organization. Without some advance insight into this work environment, and what is important to the company, your chances of winning in the interview are no greater than hitting the bullseye of a dart board at fifty paces while blindfolded. You won't even know in which direction to aim!

Having advance knowledge of the company's history, products, markets, financial performance, and the like is basic to effective interviewing. Having researched this kind of information in advance will speak volumes to the employer about your motivation, initiative, preparation, and thoroughness. It suggests that you will be equally motivated and prepared when it comes to work performance. This is certainly the kind of message that you will want the employer to get.

Too many times I have seen otherwise qualified persons show up totally unprepared for the interview. They know next to nothing about the company or its products. What kind of impression can such individuals leave? Certainly not a very good one! It makes you wonder not only about their work habits, but also about the level of their interest in employment with your company.

The purpose of this chapter is to help you understand the kind of advance research that you need to do in advance of the interview, and why it is important. Second, it is my intent to show you how to do this research—both what information it is that you need and what resources you can use to get it. Let's start first with the advance information you will need to ensure interview success.

The research you need to do in advance of the employment interview falls into three categories. These are:

1. General company information.
2. Job information.
3. Company culture/work environment.

Having key information about each of these three categories is going to be critical to conducting a successful interview as well as making the best possible employment choice. Let's systematically explore each of these to give you a full understanding of their importance.

General Company Information

As already pointed out, having advance information about the company is sure to reflect favorably on your employment candidacy. Those who take the time to carefully research the company in advance of the interview always stand out from those who don't. Their advance preparation is almost immediately evident to the interviewer, suggesting a number of positive things about their general work habits, thoroughness, motivation, and interest. Those candidates who demonstrate such positive attributes right from the beginning of the interview always stand out.

The kind of general company information that you need to research and of which you should be generally knowledgeable prior to showing up for the interview includes:

1. Company products and/or services.
2. Markets and key customers.
3. General business philosophy.
4. Short- and long-term financial performance:
   —Sales trends.
   —Cost trends.
   —Profit trends.
   —Future financial prospects.

5. Plans and strategies for growth and expansion:

—Major growth emphasis (products, divisions, etc.).

—Opportunities for growth (new or expanded markets).

—Plans for growth (e.g., new products, improved products, acquisitions, mergers, etc.).

6. Key problems and challenges:

—Internal.

—External.

Besides the general positive impression that it creates with the employer when you are knowledgeable of the company and its products, review of the above categories of information should quickly suggest to you that there are some other excellent reasons for you to engage in this kind of advance company research as well.

The first of these has to do with the company's growth and stability. If the financial data suggest that the company is in a downward spiral, does the organization offer you the kind of stability and career growth that you are seeking? How serious is this spiral? What are its causes? What is the company doing about them? What is the future prognosis, both short- and long-term? These are serious questions that should have answers before you are likely to want to cast your fate with such a shaky organization.

Beyond the advance research you have done prior to the interview, you are going to have some rather focused questions to ask of the employer during the interview discussion about the financial health of the organization. You are going to want to get a handle on how serious this problem is before you get too excited about the job opportunity this employer has to offer.

On the other hand, if the financials read well and the company is poised for explosive growth and expansion, there is probably little to concern you about the future. Instead, you are going to want to use your interview time to focus on other topics important to your career decision making.

Using your advance research to understand some of the major problems and challenges facing the employer may play to your advantage. This is particularly true if the job for which you are applying can impact on these issues, and you happen to have the right combination of knowledge and experience that could serve to help lead them out of the woods. If you have some solutions and can positively contribute to the solution of these key problems, there is likely to be significant interest in your candidacy and you are in a position to negotiate a "major league contract."

Look carefully at the company's plans and strategies for future growth and expansion. Are there areas where you could make contributions to these efforts as well? If so, you should be in a nice position to stir up some additional interest in your candidacy. Perhaps you will be in a position to share some of your ideas during your interview discussions, and stimulate increased interest in bringing you aboard.

Finally, advance research concerning the organization's overall philosophy will begin to provide you with some advance insight concerning the company's culture or work environment which, as you will see, is very important to formulating an effective interview strategy.

The single best source for much of this research is the company's annual report. A quick call to the company's Public Affairs department will normally be sufficient to speed a copy of the annual report to you. While you are at it, request product literature and any other information that might be helpful to you. This may include recent newspaper articles concerning major events affecting the company, including new product information, new divisions, mergers and acquisitions, commentary on financial performance, planned expansions, consolidations, and so on.

Also request a copy of the annual reports from the past couple of years. By reading these past issues in succession, you may be able to get a feel for changes in business and marketing strategy, new problems and challenges, or old problems that remain unresolved. This historical perspective can often prove quite helpful. Additionally, perusal of these past issues will give you a more comprehensive overview of the overall philosophy of the firm.

A trip to the local or county library may also be in order if this is a firm in which you have a strong interest. With the help of a research librarian (don't be shy about asking), you can probably use the library's online computer system and microfiche to track down articles on the company that were published in newspapers and business publications during the last two to three years. For a small investment, you are likely to walk away with an armload of good information that will prove helpful to your cause.

Another key source of information that you don't want to overlook is your stockbroker. If you have access to a large brokerage house, find out who the financial analyst is for the industry. These people are a virtual reservoir of information and can share a great deal of industry-relevant information about the company's competitive position and prognosis for success. Since they specialize in the industry, their observations can prove quite helpful.

If you have been introduced to the company through an employment agency or search firm, they can prove very helpful in helping you to acquire the kind of information that you need about the organization. Once they have interviewed you and gotten the employer to agree to an interview, they have a vested interest in seeing that things go well. Many will be glad to help at this point, so don't hesitate to ask.

Finally, don't overlook one other powerful source of information. Current employees are of tremendous value when it comes to getting the "insider perspective" of the organization. Work your social and professional contacts to see if you can get an introduction to persons now employed by your target organization. An introduction and quick phone call to these insiders can have enormous payoffs!

Job Information

Before going to the employment interview, find out as much about the job as you can. The following is a wish list of information it would be helpful to have:

Basic Information

1. Organizational chart of immediate function showing people, titles, reporting relations, and functional responsibilities.

2. Job title.

3. Your reporting relationship.

4. Size and scope of position (budget, number of people, etc.).

5. Functional responsibilities.

Nice to Have

1. Key challenges and problems.

2. Short-term objectives.

3. Long-term objectives.

4. Why position is open.

5. "Ideal candidate"—what the company really wants.

Much of the information I have classified as "basic information" is easily acquired through either the headhunter (if there is one) or the employment department of the organization. In most cases, some form of job description and organization chart can be sent to your attention, furnishing you with much of this information.

The remaining information, which I have titled "nice to have," will probably be available only through conversation with the hiring manager, the human resources department, or the headhunter. If you've not had conversations with the hiring manager (your future boss), it is best to seek this information through either the headhunter or the human resources representative, whoever has been your principal source of contact.

All of the above information will be quite helpful to you in planning your interview approach and overall strategy. This point will become even more emphatic later in the book as you begin to see the direct tie-in between this information and the kinds of questions you will be asked.

Having the luxury of knowing something about the key problems, challenges, and objectives of the position in advance of the interview discussion will give you the opportunity to thoroughly think through what you have to offer to the employer in these key areas. If you take advantage of this opportunity to carefully plan what you are going to say on these subjects, you will have a competitive advantage over others and an opportunity to enhance your value to the employer.

Company Culture/Work Environment

The final piece of company research that you are going to want to put in place, if you are going to stack the interview deck in your favor, has to do with the organization's culture or work environment. This is an area frequently overlooked by most employment candidates, yet it is highly critical to interview success.

Here are some of the components of company culture that would be enormously helpful to know something about before the interview date. As you will readily see later in the book, as we walk through the various interview questions you are likely to encounter, having advance information about the work environment will give you some strong clues as to how to answer key interview questions so as to enhance interest in your candidacy and provide you with the competitive advantage needed to win at the interview game. The key components of company culture are:

1. Overall business or management philosophy of the company:
   —Principles?
   —Values?
   —Beliefs?
2. Predominant management style:
   —Participative?
   —Controlling?
   —Other?
3. Profile of hiring manager (your future boss):
   —Traits?
   —Characteristics?
   —Principles?
   —Values?

—Beliefs?

—Management philosophy?

—Management style?

—Preferred subordinate behavior?

—Profile of "high performers" in his or her organization?

—Profile of "poor performers" in his or her organization?

Some of the general information about the company's overall business or management philosophy might be gleaned from the annual reports and newspaper clippings you have been reading. However, this is not true of some of the more specific information that you will need about the hiring manager's traits, characteristics, style, and so on. This information can only be obtained through conversation with those who are in a position to make these kinds of observations. This could include the headhunter, the human resources representative, or networking contacts now employed by the company.

Although getting information about the company culture and work environment is much harder than getting general company information and job information, it is an area that you will want to pursue if you are truly interested in the opportunity. It will be important not only to developing your specific interview strategy, but it will also be important in determining whether or not this is the kind of culture that is compatible with your own profile.

Studies have shown that the single greatest contributor to performance failure and job dissatisfaction has to do with lack of fit with organizational culture. If you don't align well with the boss's core beliefs and values, it will be very difficult to develop an effective working relationship. Because of your difference in thinking, you will probably experience trouble getting support for your ideas and the general management backing that is so important to job and career success. The net result is likely to be a great deal of discomfort and anxiety if not actual performance failure, job loss, and a severe case of depression. Life is too short, so make the extra effort to avoid this kind of potential unhappiness.

Armed with the research suggested in this chapter, you are now ready to prepare your strategy for success in the job interview. As you go along, you will see even more clearly just how valuable this advance research will be to both preparing a winning interview strategy as well as to the selection of the kind of job and work environment that you will find stimulating and rewarding. There is a lot to gain from going through this process!

2

THE INTERVIEW DAY

KNOW WHERE YOU ARE GOING

On the day of the interview, you are going to want to arrive at least 15 minutes early. Leave plenty of extra time for any contingencies such as traffic delays, getting a cab, and so on, that could cause you to arrive late and create a lot of unnecessary stress and anxiety. The last thing you need is to arrive late, out-of-breath, disheveled, with heart palpitating and sweat running down your forehead. This is not the recommended way to get the employment interview off to a good start!

This means first and foremost that you need to know where it is that you are going. As simplistic as this idea may sound, while working as an employment manager at Scott Paper Company's corporate headquarters in Philadelphia, I remember a sales candidate who was late for his interview appointment and who frantically called to say that he had mistakenly thought that the company's headquarters was in Pittsburgh. He was calling from the Pittsburgh International Airport. Guess who didn't get the job, let alone the interview?

Although I'm sure you wouldn't do anything quite this bad, be sure you know where you are going. Get *explicit* directions ahead of time so that you know not only where the interview is to take place, but exactly how to get there. If it is a local interview, and you are not familiar with the specific area, it's probably a good idea to do a "dry run" and drive there the day before the interview. In this way, you will be sure that there will be no confusion and that you will be able to arrive on time and in the right frame of mind.

PROPER DRESS AND APPEARANCE

A lot has been written about proper attire and appearance for the employment interview. The standard recommendation is:

- *For Men: Most literature recommends that men arrive for the employment interview in either a navy blue or grey suit, white dress shirt, and conservative tie. Shoes should be black and well-shined. Clothing should be clean, crisp, well-pressed, and properly fitted. Hair should be well-groomed, not too long, and neatly trimmed. Avoid unusual or gaudy jewelry and, if you wear them, remove those earrings!*
- *For Women: The usual recommendations for women include a navy, grey, or subdued color suit/blazer and skirt, and appropriately coordinated accessories. Go easy on the jewelry, makeup, and perfume!*

Although generally these are the dress rules, and have been for some time, the new, more relaxed dress codes of certain companies may allow something that is a little less formal. However, to be on the safe side, you are still probably better off to follow the conventional wisdom and stick with the traditional interview attire.

THE GREETING

A lot has also been written over the years about the proper way to greet your interviewer and the importance of first impressions. Much of this conventional wisdom still applies. The initial impression you create could well be a lasting one, so make it good!

Your greeting should be pleasant and cordial. A warm smile, firm handshake, and good eye contact will go a long way in creating that favorable first impression. Thank your host or hostess for the opportunity to be there and express your positive enthusiasm for the day that lies ahead. Here is an example of what you might say:

Good morning, Sandra, I'm Steve Jordan. Thanks for the opportunity to visit with you today. I'm really looking forward to discussing the opportunity to work as a project engineer in your Technology Department. From what I have been told by the search firm, it sounds like an interesting position.

As you enter your host's office, wait until asked to be seated. Upon invitation, say "thank you" and be seated at the designated place.

Although it should almost go without saying, do not light up a cigarette or chew gum during the interview. Both are considered inappropriate if not offensive behavior. You seriously jeopardize the interview if you disregard this advice.

BODY LANGUAGE

Be conscious of your physical appearance and body language throughout the interview discussion. Maintain erect but not "ram rod" posture during the discussion. Good posture signals the interviewer that you are energetic and interested in the discussion.

Do not slouch down in the chair. If you are too relaxed, this may suggest to the employer that you are lazy, lack energy and motivation, or are just plain disinterested in the conversation at hand. None of these will help your cause.

Conversely, avoid sitting too rigidly in the chair, which may suggest that you are very formal, distant, unfriendly, or possibly even aloof. Sitting on the edge of your chair may suggest that you are nervous, tense, or high-strung, where leaning forward toward the interviewer and invading his or her personal space could be interpreted as a very aggressive or confrontive style.

Maintain good eye contact throughout the interview. Looking the interviewer in the eye conveys a sense of openness, honesty, self-confidence, and interest. Although eye contact should be good, avoid staring too intensely as if trying to stare your interviewer down. This might signal overly aggressive or even hostile behavior.

Lack of good eye contact can have a detrimental effect. Looking down suggests someone who is shy and lacking in self-confidence. On the other hand, looking away may suggest to the employer that you are shifty, sneaky, closed, dishonest, or worse.

Avoid unconscious nervous motions. Tapping your pencil, stroking your hair, rubbing your ears, grinding your teeth, picking your fingernails, rubbing your nose, frequently adjusting glasses, stroking your tie, and so on, all have no place in the interview. Such actions are disconcerting and distract the interviewer's attention away from what you are saying, calling attention to your nervous actions. This could subtract substantially from your overall presentation.

Avoid the tendency to talk too much with your hands. I have interviewed people who so overused hand gesturing that I felt that perhaps I was interviewing the maestro from the Philadelphia Orchestra. This too will draw attention away from your message, as the interviewer sits there waiting for the concert to start.

PRESENTATION STYLE

Your presentation style should connote energy and enthusiasm. Avoid using a monotone, as this can be deadly and even put people to sleep. Instead, vary the tone and speed of your speech to create interest and emphasize key points you wish to make.

Show your excitement and enthusiasm for those aspects of the job or work environment that sound particularly interesting and grab your attention. Words like, "that sounds exciting," "that's really interesting," etc., will show that you're alive, interested, enthused, and even excited with what is being presented to you. Showing such interest and excitement suggests to the employer that you are stimulated and motivated to perform the kind of work they have to offer. All things being otherwise equal, enthusiasm can be a big tie-breaker when it comes to the employer picking one candidate over another. I've seen it happen a number of times. As the saying goes, "Enthusiasm is contagious!"

Be attentive and listen carefully to what is being said in the interview. Good listening skills are paramount to effective communications and interpersonal relations. This skill will not go unnoticed by the employer.

Good presentation style requires that you be persuasive and convincing in the points you make. Broad, flowery statements about your capabilities without specific examples to back it up, will soon sound shallow, self-serving, and totally unconvincing. Thorough interview preparation is the cornerstone for establishing credibility with the interviewer.

Finally, a warm, friendly, open style will go a long way toward building good rapport, and a feeling that you would be an enjoyable person to have around and to work with.

COMMUNICATION SKILLS

The following listing will help get the message across concerning what is important to effective communication skills, if you are to create a favorable impression in the interview:

Expressive (alive, animated speech).

Articulate (words clearly pronounced).

Concise (not too wordy or rambling).

Focused (to-the-point).

Direct (straightforward, not evasive).

There is a lot to consider during the interview day, if you are going to maximize the opportunity and increase the probability of walking away with a job offer. Certainly the need to practice your interviewing skills should be readily apparent to those who are really serious about getting that job offer.

But all of these things are for naught unless you are fully prepared and have a well thought-out strategy for handling the myriad of questions and situations presented by the interviewer. The balance of this book should go a long way in helping you to put it all together.

3

FIVE WINNING
INTERVIEW
STRATEGIES

O ver the years I have been privileged to be a participant in numerous employment interviews of candidates for a wide range of positions, from entry-level, hourly factory workers to corporation presidents. For the first nine years of my human resources career, which was with Scott Paper Company, I worked in manufacturing plants, where I was engaged in interviewing and hiring hundreds of workers for hourly mill positions. Later, while in a human resources generalist role for one of the company's small divisions, I was accountable for all salaried employment, both professional and managerial, for the full range of business functions—sales and marketing, manufacturing operations, technical, accounting, human resources. Still later, as technical employment manager at Scott's corporate offices, I was responsible for hiring technical professional and managerial personnel for the research and development and central engineering functions, as well as providing support to some 13 manufacturing sites in the recruitment and employment of operations management and technical support personnel (mostly engineers).

After resigning from Scott Paper, I accepted a position as vice president and consultant with a major international executive search firm. Employment experience here was focused on high-level managers and executives for a whole host of companies in a variety of industries. This included some international recruiting and employment assignments as well.

Although I have never taken the time to do an actual count, I would not be surprised to find that during my last nearly 30 years of employment-related experience, I have interviewed as many as two thousand people. Needless to say, I have had plenty of opportunity to personally observe a huge number of employment candidates of all shapes and sizes engaged in the interview process—both good and bad.

In this chapter, I am going to share with you some observations that I have made about persons who really stood out during the interview process. These were the candidates about whom, before the interview day was complete and the candidate had left for home, I would get a call from the hiring manager saying, with excitement and enthusiasm, "We need to make an offer to Sally before she leaves today! She's exactly what we're looking for, and we want her to know that we are really interested in having her join our department!"

Calls of this type were infrequent but when, as the employment manager, you received them, you knew that you had a real "live wire" on your hands. It was also a clear signal that this was an employment candidate who had interviewed extremely well—someone who had done something special in the interview to warrant this level of excitement.

In most cases, the company had interviewed a half dozen or so candidates for the same position with only a modicum of interest, but none had created anywhere near the level of enthusiasm and excitement that Sally did. What had Sally done differently from others in the interview to generate this level of excitement? Clearly, she had stumbled onto something that had really "turned the crank" of the interview team. What was it?

By remembering back on other candidates who, like Sally, had stimulated considerable interest in their candidacy, it occurred to me that there were some common threads that seemed to account for their interviewing success. What were these? By observing these commonalities, perhaps it would be possible to "package" these as key interviewing strategies and pass them along to others as techniques for creating a competitive advantage in the interview process that would allow these persons to shine over less knowledgeable candidates.

It was this kind of rhetorical questioning that caused me to realize that there was a very definite pattern of a handful of interview strategies employed (knowingly or unknowingly) by these outstanding candidates that made them stand out so vividly when compared to their competition. In this chapter, I share these winning strategies with you, and teach you how to employ them to create a high level of excitement about your own employment candidacy.

The ideas or strategies in this chapter are more than just theory. As part of my outplacement consulting practice, I have trained hundreds in the use of these interviewing techniques and have had the chance to witness, on a first-hand basis, just how powerful these techniques can be when used effectively by those going through the job search process. I have witnessed numerous individuals return from the employment interview to provide strong testimony on how use of one or another of these techniques was just the thing that served to turn the interview around in its tracks and generate strong interest in their employment candidacy.

THE "PERFECT CANDIDATE" STRATEGY

The first of these interview strategies is known as the "perfect candidate" strategy. To employ this strategy, the employment candidate simply asks the hiring manager (i.e., the person who would be their boss in the new position) to describe the "perfect candidate" for the position.

Here are some ways this might be done:

- *How would you describe the perfect candidate for this position?*

- *What do you feel are the ideal qualifications for this job?*

- *What factors do you feel are most important for success in this position?*

- *As you think about past persons who have been very successful in this job, in your judgment what factors most contributed to their success?*

Of these approaches, I would strongly recommend the third. Asking about the factors thought to be important to successful performance of the job is really the same thing as asking the hiring manager to describe the "perfect or ideal" candidate for the job, but it is far less obvious.

In most cases, if you were to ask a seasoned interviewer to describe the perfect candidate for the job, you are likely not to have this question answered. Experienced interviewers will studiously avoid telegraphing the profile of the ideal candidate they are seeking. They are avoiding providing you with the "answers to the exam" ahead of time. By letting you in on the secret ahead of time allows you the opportunity to slant your answers to interview questions so as to resemble this ideal candidate profile. By sharing this desired profile with you, the interviewer has biased your answers in favor of this profile and therefore does not have the opportunity to get an objective reading on your qualifications and fit for the position.

In such cases, the skillful interviewer will politely avoid answering your rather direct question, and you are bound to get an answer similar to the following: "Jim, I'd be glad to answer your question about the perfect candidate for this position, but first I think it is important for me to learn more about you. Perhaps we can return to your question a little later in the interview."

Instead of being so direct, it is better to be a little less obvious as to what you are up to. Rather than ask directly for a description of the "perfect or ideal candidate" for the position, try asking about those factors the hiring manager feels are going to be most important to success in the job. This is truly the same question as the "ideal candidate" approach, but it is far less obvious to the interviewer. Most interviewers will be only too glad to share what they feel will be important to success in the position. After all, they are just as concerned about the potential for successful performance of the position as you are.

If you are successful in getting the employer to answer this question, which in many cases you will be, you have provided yourself with an enormous competitive advantage in the interview. This is particularly true if you ascertain what this "success profile" looks like near the beginning of the interview.

In understanding what the interviewer feels is required for successful job performance early in the interview conversation, you now have a clear understanding of what specific qualifications (i.e., knowledge, skills, abilities, competencies, traits, characteristics) the employer is seeking and will motivate the hiring manger to make an employment offer. Your job becomes a lot easier since you can now zero in on these qualifications that you know are important to the hiring manager's making a positive hiring decision.

This is tantamount to having the answers to the final exam ahead of time. All you need to do at this point is to "parrot" back what the interviewer has told you was important to performance success, describing yourself as the ideal candidate for the position.

In sales parlance, this is known as "qualifying the buyer." Successful sales professionals have long known that unless you "qualify" the buyer at the beginning of the sales presentation (i.e., get the buyer to articulate what is important to making a positive buying decision), there is little chance that you will make the sale. Without this knowledge you are "shooting in the dark" and making the sale is strictly a "hit or miss" proposition.

You have probably been in the position of observing a salesperson make an excellent sales presentation but not walk away with the sale. In these cases, the individual may do an outstanding job of describing all of the various important attributes and benefits of the product, and drone on and on but never once stop to determine what aspects of the product are of most importance to the potential buyer. The result may be that the single most important factor that would motivate this buyer to purchase the product is simply overlooked by the sales representative, and the bottom-line result is "no sale."

The same thing is true of successful interviewing. After all, the employment interview is in fact a selling situation. Only, in this case, the product is you! Unless you are successful in qualifying the buyer (i.e., the hiring manager) and determining what is important to that manager's employment decision, there's not much likelihood of your making the sale.

If you are going to stack the interview deck in your favor, the perfect candidate strategy has to become an important item in your bag of winning interview tricks.

THE "PERFORMANCE IMPROVEMENT" STRATEGY

Through the process of observing highly successful employment candidates interview, another technique that I have seen many of them employ is what I call the "performance improvement" strategy. This is a somewhat simple but highly effective interview technique.

At the heart of this strategy is the natural desire for the hiring manager to want to hire someone who can perform the job better than the last person who held the position. No matter how good this person was, there is always the opportunity for some improvement in overall job performance. The objective of this interview technique is to discover where these opportunities for improved performance lay.

Here are some questions you can use during the interview discussion to determine what these areas for performance improvement are:

- *Jane, as you think about how this job has been performed by others in the past, where do you feel there are opportunities for improvement? And, what kind of improvement would you most like to see?*

- *In the context of overall department success, what aspects of this position would you most like to see improved from a performance standpoint?*

- *If you could change something about how this position has been performed in the past, what would it be and what improvement would you most like to see?*

It's axiomatic that all managers want to see performance improvement in their organizations. Further, they want to feel that the person they select as a candidate for the position they are attempting to fill will bring the ability to upgrade performance of both the job and the department. After all, in addition to taking some of the load off the manager's shoulders, any overall performance improvement is going to make the manager look good as well. Such improvement has a way of positively impacting important factors such as the manager's own performance evaluation and salary increases—topics that are near and dear to heart of any self-respecting executive.

Answers to questions such as those cited, will provide you with a competitive interview advantage if you are clever enough and quick enough on your feet to turn these answers into an advantage. The obvious approach is to talk about those skills and abilities that will enable you to bring improved performance to those aspects of the job that have been singled out by the hiring manager as representing opportunities for overall improvement. Convincing the manager that you can bring about the desired improvement will go a long way toward assuring the manager that you will bring an added measure of value to the organization, and that you are well worth hiring over other candidates under consideration for the position.

THE "STRATEGIC OBJECTIVES" TECHNIQUE

My first-hand observations of numerous employment interviews has served to make me keenly aware that a great deal of the employment interview (probably 95 percent or better) focuses on the existing job as it is currently performed. Watching the pattern of interview questions in the great majority of interviews will quickly convince you that this observation is right on target.

What typically occurs is a scenario where the hiring manager and interview team focus almost exclusively on examining and evaluating the candidate's ability to perform the key elements of the job. The candidate will be asked a long series of specific questions about his or her ability to solve certain types of problems required for successful performance of the principal accountabilities of the position. Thus, the great bulk of the interview tends to focus on the candidate's "technical" qualifications for the position. The interview team wants to know whether or not the candidate has the specialized knowledge and abilities to successfully perform these important job elements.

Surprisingly, most interviews are so focused on examining the "here and now" (i.e., the job as it now exists) that seldom is there ever any attention given to some of the longer term strategic changes that the person will be required to bring about as a result of the need to support the long-term strategic goals of the organization. Hence, the average employment candidate will be content to confine conversation and descriptions of his or her capabilities to these more immediate, near-term needs.

Here's where my skills as an observer of employment interview history can have some real payoff for those who are willing to step out of the ordinary and display a real ability for strategic leadership. Are you listening?

What tipped me off to the power of this particular interview strategy was the recollection that several of the high-powered candidates I have observed had discovered that by shifting the focus of the interview discussion from the current job to business strategy provided them with an opportunity to put some competitive distance between themselves and other candidates for the same position. My clue to picking up on this particular phenomenon was remembering those several cases where I would receive a call from the hiring manager, who would enthusiastically say something similar to the following:

Dick, I just finished interviewing Dave Jackson, and I've got to tell you that I am really impressed. We should try to get him an offer before he leaves here today. Not

*only can he do a good job for us in the current position,
but he can help us with our need to automate the bot-
tling line. This is something that we really need to be
doing.*

Okay, you be the detective. What is really going on here?
What has this candidate probably done that others, who
had been interviewed for the same position, didn't? Exactly
what created this kind of enthusiasm for Dave's candidacy,
when others could not even raise so much as a single goose
bump of excitement? Give up?

Well, in case you missed the point, the answer is that
Dave not only convinced the interview team that he had the
"right stuff" to perform the regular job, but he also convinced them that he had the ability to help the group to
achieve one of its longer term objectives—something they
hadn't even thought about until he uncovered the need.
This served to create a sense of "added value" about his capability, and distinguished him from the other candidates
who had been interviewed for the same position.

These observations have led me to the conclusion that, as
an employment candidate, you can normally generate considerable interest in candidacy by framing yourself as a
"positive change agent"—one who is concerned, beyond the
current job, in bringing longer term strategic change and
improvement to the organization.

In this age of downsized organizations, where the emphasis is on doing more, better, and with fewer resources
(especially people), it should not surprise you to find that
organizations have a keen interest in those who have this
kind of forward-thinking, strategic focus. Sometimes in
the heat of the employment interview, however, the importance of longer term strategy is lost in the rush to better
understand how well the candidate can perform the immediate job—get their hands around the immediate needs and
wrestle those current, nagging problems that occupy so
much of the daily routine, to the ground.

Before the interview team realizes it, time has run out
and it's time to run the candidate on to the next appointed
interview station. Unfortunately, if it was planned at
all, there was no time remaining to probe the candidate's

ability to help with some of the department's longer term goals. Although most may not like to admit it, in more cases than not the hiring manager and interview team have been so busy and preoccupied with doing their current jobs (especially in the downsized environment where time is at a premium) that little if any advance thought has been given to the longer term strategic needs of the organization.

These very same individuals, given only a minimum of gentle prodding, would likely freely admit that more time and advance preparation should have been given to these strategic issues. Most would readily admit that gauging the candidate's ability to help drive the strategic changes needed by the organization deserved far more attention than was provided—a sad but true admission.

This significant omission can often play right into the hands of the astute employment candidate, if equipped (with the right interview strategy) to fully exploit the situation. Here is where the "strategic objectives" interview strategy, if well executed, has the potential to put miles between you and your competition for the same job.

The process for implementing this technique is fairly basic and, with a little thought, fairly obvious. The intent of this strategy is, first, to gain some fundamental insight about the department's longer term strategy and goals, and then to ask some fairly direct questions about the impact of these strategic objectives on the position for which you are being considered. Specifically, what changes or improvements are you going to need to bring about as the job incumbent in order to help the department (and the organization) to achieve its longer term goals and satisfy its future requirement?

Here are some approaches you can use to refocus the interview team or hiring manager's attention away from immediate job demands to these more strategic issues:

- *Mary, as you think about some of the organization's longer term goals and objectives, what are some of the changes and improvements that are going to be needed to be brought about in this position in order to realize these goals?*

- *How do the organization's longer term goals impact this job? What are some of the longer term strategic improvements that you would like to see made by a successful candidate for this position?*
- *How does this position tie in with some of the company's intermediate and long-term objectives? What strategic changes and improvements are going to be important to successful job performance from your perspective?*

From previous discussion, the potency of this particular interview strategy should, by now, be quite evident. By determining what is desired in the way of strategic changes to the job the way it is currently performed, the employment candidate has the perfect opportunity to "frame" himself or herself as just the positive change agent to bring these improvements about!

Here are some questions you can use to probe the subject even further and gain even clearer insight into what the strategic needs of the job are:

- *What do you currently see as the major barriers to bringing these strategic changes about?*
- *What key problems need to be solved in order to move successfully ahead toward these goals?*
- *What do you believe needs to be done to move ahead on this strategic front?*

By asking these kinds of questions during the interview, you are providing a gentle reminder to the hiring manager of the need to look at your qualifications to do the longer term strategic things as well as meet the short-term, obvious needs of the job. Simply demonstrating your interest in such strategic matters will often set you apart from the other candidates.

Such strategic focus says something to the hiring manager (your future boss) about your commitment to the future and desire to help bring about continuous improvement to the organization. This begins to silently speak "tons" about your motivation and desire to take initiative—characteristics that will set you apart from your competition and create that sense of "added value" about your employment candidacy. What hiring manager wouldn't want to hire someone who is capable of performing the immediate job, but who is also motivated to continuously look for ways that things can be improved and done better?

Finally, in this world of downsized organizations and limited resources, there is a big drive afoot on the part of most companies to pursue a "total quality" initiative designed to satisfy the customers (both inside and outside the organization). This drive is based on the fundamental idea of "do it right the first time." Doing so assures complete customer satisfaction, promotes efficiency, and eliminates wasted resources.

An underlying principle embedded in this approach is the idea of continuous improvement. Much of today's corporate energy is focused on linking these two ideas—using complete customer satisfaction as the ultimate goal and continuous improvement efforts as the vehicle for achieving this worthy objective. Thus there is a predisposition toward continuous improvement, and employment candidates who are strategically focused and motivated toward continuous improvement are very much in demand by the modern organization. The "strategic objective" interview strategy, as described here, is thus one that fits the times and should enhance interest in one's employment candidacy.

Now you have one more valuable tool for your interview success tool kit. What else can you do to create special interest in your employment candidacy and beat the competition?

THE "KEY PROBLEMS" STRATEGY

As I often tell students in my classes on interviewing techniques, "The only reason why jobs exist is that problems exist. If organizations didn't have problems that needed to be solved, there would be no need for people to solve them, and thus no jobs to be filled." If "problem solution" is the fundamental underlying reason for the existence of jobs, then doesn't it make sense that the ability to solve problems will be, in large measure, the focal point of much of job interview discussion?

As you think about the various interviews of which you have been part, either as an employer or as a candidate, you will probably quickly identify with the statement that a good part of the interview discussion is focused entirely on the candidate's ability to successfully solve certain key problems normally associated with successful performance of the job. If interviewing a candidate for the position of employment manager, for example, what can the candidate do to improve or upgrade the quality of persons hired by the business? This begins to drive into areas such as the candidate's specific interviewing and evaluation skills. What evidence can be seen that the candidate has the skills and ability to solve the problem of better selection?

Problem solving is a fundamental focal point of the interview process and will be key to a candidate's interviewing success. The ability to solve the key problems must take center stage from the candidate's interview strategy standpoint. Realizing this in advance of the interview has the potential to empower the employment candidate right from the start and provide a competitive advantage in the interview.

Observation of "heavy hitters" in the interview process has led me to the conclusion that most of them innately realize the importance of problem solving as perhaps the key point of distinction between successful candidates and those who fail to get the job offer. Those who are able to demonstrate competence in their ability to solve the problems associated with successful job performance will be the winners. Those who apparently lack competence in these important areas will lose.

Successful interviewees are those who are quick to focus interview attention on their "technical competence" to solve these key problems and achieve the results expected of them in the job's major areas of functional accountability. In fact, they can hardly wait for the interview to get started so they can demonstrate their technical (i.e., problem-solving) competence to perform the work in question.

As a candidate, particularly if well-qualified, you will want the interview to get to the problem-solving component at the earliest opportunity so that you will have ample opportunity to demonstrate competence in these important areas within the time allotted to the interview discussion. By allowing the interview to "float" too much, especially where the interviewer is particularly unskilled and lacks focus, there is always the danger that time will run out before you have been able to demonstrate your job qualifications.

In this case, you will need to be prepared to take charge of the interview (in an appropriate, non-offensive way), and refocus discussion on those areas important to proper selection. Allowing the interviewer to engage in too much discussion about his or her golf game or your skills as a captain of your 36-foot sailboat, is simply not going to help you make the sale—unless, of course, you are interviewing for the position of golf pro or ship's captain.

Actually, without being offensive, the sooner you can get the conversation directed to your key problem-solving abilities, the better. You will simply buy more time for "making your case" and also allow some extra time to explore the position's strategic needs, as discussed earlier.

The following are some ways to rapidly transition interview focus on your technical competence and your problem-solving abilities:

- *As you think about this position, what are some of the key problems you would most like to see tackled by a new person in this job?*

- *What fundamental problems do you feel a successful candidate for this position will need to be able to solve?*

- *If it were a year from now and a person had been particularly successful in this job, what things would be different from the way they are today? What key problems would have been solved?*

As you study these questions, you can begin to get a keen sense of just how potent this particular interview strategy might be. By asking these kinds of questions early in the interview, you will not only get the interview on track a lot sooner but will also provide yourself with a huge competitive advantage.

Answers to these questions will provide you with considerable insight about what is truly important to the hiring manager. Not only will you better understand the basic challenges of the job, but you will have a crystal clear understanding about the hiring manager's priorities as well. These are areas that you know are most important to the hiring manager—because he or she told you so!!

Less skilled candidates will never have this kind of opportunity. Without understanding the manager's most pressing issues, there will be a tendency to talk on and on about skills and capabilities that, although interesting, have little bearing on what is really important to that hiring manager's desire to hire you.

In contrast, by framing the manager's most pressing problems and concerns early in the interview, and by gaining further insight as to why these are areas of concern, you will be in a far better position to discuss relevant qualifications that suggest that you can really provide meaningful help in these important areas of need. Also, if asked early enough in the interview, you can buy yourself some additional time to give quality thought to viable solutions to these issues and can return to these areas of interest later in the interview discussion when the opportunity presents itself.

This type of strategy, if well-executed, can provide you with a very real competitive advantage in the interview. But what other techniques might also prove helpful?

THE "KEY CHALLENGES" STRATEGY

This particular strategy is a close cousin to the "key problems" interview strategy just discussed, but with a minor twist. Although there is not a lot of difference between the term "challenges" and the term "problems" from the interviewing standpoint, the difference is similar to what might be described as the difference in meaning between the terms "problems" and "opportunities." For the optimist, "problems" are "opportunities," where for the pessimist, "problems" are nothing less than a "pain in the neck."

The basic difference between this approach and the "key problems" strategy is a matter of tone rather than any real substance. Use of the words "challenge" or "opportunity" simply has a more positive ring than asking about "problems"—which imparts a more negative connotation.

Here's how the "key challenges" strategy might be introduced by you into the interview conversation:

- *What do you feel are some of the major challenges to be faced in this job?*
- *What do you visualize as the major opportunity areas for this position?*
- *From an improvement standpoint, where do you feel the major challenges of this position lay?*

Although at first you may see little difference between this and the "key problems" strategy, and admittedly there probably is very little, it is interesting to see the effects that use of different terms can have on the thinking process. The subtle difference in meaning between the terms "challenges" and "problems" may be just enough to elicit an entirely different response from the hiring manager.

For example, when asking the hiring manager about "key problems," he or she may cite the need for cost containment or the need to reduce headcount. When asked about challenges or opportunities, however, the same manager might mention the opportunity to influence thinking on some major piece of business strategy, or the challenge of finding ways of linking human resources planning with business strategy.

As you can see, there is some subtle difference between these two approaches, and using the "key challenges" or "key opportunities" strategy (the two are interchangeable) may serve to provide you with further important insights about what the hiring manager sees as important to successful job performance. Talking about what you would do to seize these challenges and exploit these opportunities could just be the ticket to a good job offer. At the very least, it will provide you with greater depth of understanding about the job requirements than most candidates will acquire, and provide you with yet another tool for gaining an advantage over competition for the position.

There is much you can do from a strategy standpoint to favorably influence the outcome of the employment interview by using a little creativity and resourcefulness. You now have the toolbox to build some distance between you and your competition. All you have to do is practice using each of these strategic tools to become a skilled interviewee.

4

DAMAGE CONTROL
IN THE INTERVIEW

There you are in the middle of the job interview and you have that terrible sinking feeling that things are rapidly spiraling down the tubes and there's not a thing that you can do to stop it. There's that sick feeling in the pit of your stomach that you have just said something that you knew was going to be a "show stopper." You are out of control and in that irreversible kamikaze tailspin that spells certain disaster.

Sound familiar? For most it does. If you're one of those superhuman individuals who has managed to escape the mortal bonds of human frailty, however, you've missed one of life's truly exhilarating experiences—"death by interview"!! For those of us who have been there, it's truly a humbling experience. Few things can quite compare.

THE KILLER QUESTION

Invariably it all starts with that one killer question—that one dreaded question that you hoped you wouldn't have to answer—that one question that you hoped the interviewer would forget to ask (but knew in your heart he wouldn't)— "What are your weaknesses?"

There is probably no other question in an interviewer's repertoire that causes as much anxiety or outright panic as this one. And, there is perhaps no more deadly question than this one for those who are unprepared to answer it.

Okay, we've identified the problem, now what do we do about it? Believe it or not, there are some great strategies for dealing with negative information in the interview. These are time-proven techniques that work, and have the potential, if well-executed, to keep things headed in a positive direction. This is what is known as "damage control in the interview"—the subject of this important chapter.

THE SUBTLE APPROACH

Actually, employers are a bit more subtle than I just implied. Most won't approach this delicate area quite so abruptly. The great majority will not simply blurt right out, "What are your weaknesses?" Instead, they will attempt to be a little more subtle and sensitive to your feelings than this.

The point is, however, that from the employer's viewpoint a key objective of the interview discussion is to discover your weaknesses or shortcomings and to be sure that none of these will prove fatal from a job performance standpoint. The interview process after all is every much a "screening out" process as it is a "screening in" or selection process. This means that the employer is continuously attempting to screen out those perceived to have problems or flaws in favor of those who appear to represent a lower level of employment risk.

Keeping this in mind, it is important to understand that the employer will consciously devote a reasonably-sized portion of the interview to this area of discomfort. Most realize that there is no such thing as the perfect candidate. There will invariably be an area or two where the candidate is going to be something less than the ideal match for the position. In such cases, the questions for the employer become: "Just how important is this shortcoming? Is it a minor concern, or is it something important that will severely limit the candidate's ability (or motivation) to perform the job?" These are the questions that are very much on the employer's mind, and rightfully so.

This matter of "weaknesses" is a difficult one to define from the interview standpoint. What may be considered to be a strength with one employer might well be considered a weakness by another. For example, for one manager being "strong analytically" may be viewed as a strength if the interviewing manager is one who is cautious by nature. However, a manager who prides himself or herself as being a "real entrepreneurial risk-taker" may see this same "strongly analytical" person as being a probable detriment to organizational success. Such persons might be viewed, in this case, as "overly cautious," "indecisive," or "lacking a sense of urgency."

This issue of "weaknesses" is far more subtle than you might first think. To some extent, it's like mercury—it's hard to get your fingers around it. The rules of the game will change from job to job and from employer to employer. What is seen as a strength for one job opportunity will be seen as a weakness for another. What is seen as a weakness in one work environment will be viewed as a strength in another. As the saying goes, "Beauty is in the eye of the beholder." It depends on who is doing the interviewing, and what they feel is important. There are no "absolutes" in the interview process.

In the interview game, we seem to be playing on a tilted Ouija board. Things seem to move all over the place without a sense of definitive direction or control. How then, under these conditions, can we win at the interview game? When a weakness is a strength and a strength is a weakness, how is it possible to come out on the winning side of the equation? How, under these conditions, does one exercise "damage control" in the interview?

Believe it or not, there are some good answers to these questions! If you are smart enough at playing the interview game, there are ways to gain the upper hand. Even under these circumstances, if you are thoughtful and clever at how you go about it, you can more consistently than not come out a winner. It's all in how you play the game.

From the candidate's perspective, the answer to winning the interview has a lot to do with the difference between "damage control" and "evasive action." In damage control, the ship has already been hit and the objective is to minimize the damage. "Evasive action," on the other hand, is intended to avoid the hit in the first place. Evasive action is a type of planned, purposeful preventive action designed to avoid the bombs and torpedoes that will sink your ship.

By "evasive," I don't mean that you are to avoid answering the employer's questions or that you are to become deceitful or dishonest in your response. Such strategies are bound to fail. Instead, what I mean is that you have to be smart in how you go about answering those difficult questions. Your answers need to be thought out in advance of the interview; they need to be carefully crafted to avoid taking a "direct hit" and specifically designed to minimize potential damage.

Before you can set up a good defensive strategy to avoid a "direct hit" during the interview, you have to first understand something about the employer's most probable plan of attack. If you have no advance intelligence, you are going blindly into the heat of the battle without a defined defensive strategy, and are therefore totally at the mercy of the interviewer. In such cases, there is a "high probability" that you are going to experience a sudden surprise attack, sustain several direct hits, and the ship will be sinking before you even know that you've been hit.

It has long been said that "the best defense is a good offense," and this applies to the art of interviewing as well. If you're planning to win, you can't just sit back and wait for the opponent to score the first points. If you do, the first thing you know is that the opposing team is three touchdowns ahead, and the game's outcome is in serious jeopardy. If the game is interviewing, this is likely to equate to a losing margin and you might as well call a "forfeiture," take your bag, and go on home.

If you're going to win at interviewing, you've got to *plan* to win. You have to have a both a strategy and a plan for winning. But even before you can formulate such a plan, you must first have some basic intelligence about the opponent. What weapons are they carrying and what is the most probable plan of attack?

To defeat the enemy, we must first think like the enemy. We must know what their current position is, what their objectives are, what weapons they have, how they will most likely use them, the direction of attack, the mode of attack, and their overall battle strategy.

We will first start with understanding how the employer thinks. This will give you some strong clues on what they are likely to do, and what you will need to do, in turn, to successfully counter their action and both design and execute a winning interview strategy.

EMPLOYER'S PLAN OF ATTACK

Throughout the interview, the employer will be constantly on the lookout for any negative patterns or trends that begin to emerge as the interview moves along. These are the factors that, if serious, the employer will latch onto as the basis for not selecting the candidate and sending the infamous "no thank you" letter.

Having observed and participated directly in thousands of employment interviews over my professional lifetime, I can tell you with a high level of confidence that most employment interviews tend to be "highly predictable." Close observation shows that, in a high percentage of cases, employers have a tendency to focus on the same half-dozen areas as the basis for selection of candidates, and there is a distinct pattern to the questions they tend to ask.

As the employer plans the interview strategy, therefore, there will be a series of areas that are most likely to be probed, as a matter of course, to determine if the candidate will fit both the job and the work environment. Here are the areas normally targeted for evaluation and some of the typical questions floating through the employer's mind as he or she begins to formulate a basic interview design:

Technical Competence

- Are there any indications that the candidate lacks the necessary knowledge and skills to perform the key elements of the job?
- If there are skill or knowledge deficits, how serious are they?
- Is there any evidence that suggests that there are elements of this job that the candidate will be unable to perform?
- What does the candidate's past performance history tell us about how well the person will (or will not) perform?
- In past performance evaluations, what were the areas mentioned as areas needing improvement or personal development?
- Is there an historical trend? Has there been some pattern to these improvement need areas?
- Are any of these improvement need areas critical to successful performance of the job?
- How serious is the problem? What is the level of risk?

Job Motivation

- How motivated is the candidate to perform this kind of work?
- Does evidence exist that this type of job is something that the employment candidate will find less than stimulating?
- Has the candidate performed similar work in the past?
- How did he or she feel about this work?
- What aspects did he or she dislike? How much?

- How will this impact his or her motivation to perform this work?

Fit with Work Environment

- How well will the candidate fit into our work environment?
- Are there aspects of our work environment that will cause problems?
- How serious will this incompatibility be? Serious? Not so serious?
- In what past work environments has the candidate not been happy?
- Why? What factors caused this unhappiness?
- Are those same factors present in our work environment?
- Will this seriously jeopardize the candidate's ability to fit in and perform?

Fit with Boss

- How compatible will the candidate be with the boss's management philosophy and style?
- Will the candidate be compatible or incompatible with the boss?
- Where is the potential for incompatibility?
- Were there past bosses with whom the candidate was incompatible?
- Why? What was the source of the incompatibility?
- What aspects of the boss' philosophy or style caused the discomfort?
- Is there a similar trend with other bosses for whom the candidate worked?
- How similar (or dissimilar) is the new boss' philosophy/style to those with whom the candidate has been least compatible?

- How serious is this incompatibility? Serious? Not so serious?
- What impact is this incompatibility likely to have on job performance?

Interpersonal Relationships

- What has been the candidate's past history in the area of interpersonal relationships?
- Has he or she generally gotten along well with others?
- Has there been any kind of history of not getting along well with others?
- With whom? What were the circumstances?
- With what kinds of persons has the candidate not normally gotten along? What is characteristic of these people?
- Will the candidate need to work with people of this type in the new work environment?
- Are these critical working relationships from a job performance standpoint?
- How will the candidate react? What will he or she do?
- How serious will this be from a job performance standpoint? Serious? Not so serious?

Past Failures

- What other factors have influenced work performance in the past?
- What past work experience has been a failure or disappointment?
- What factors influenced this failure or disappointment?
- Has there been a pattern or trend of similar failures or disappointments?
- Are any of these factors present in this job or work environment?

- How will this impact the candidate's ability or desire to perform?

As you can see from review of these key focus areas and related lists of questions, when designing interviews, employers are very much focused on examining the candidate's qualifications in three primary areas: technical competency, motivation to do the work, and fit with the organization's culture or work environment. It should also be evident from these questions that employers will focus a good part of their interview time on attempting to discover the candidate's shortcomings and assessing the degree of performance risk associated with each.

Being able to confidently and comfortably handle "negative information" about yourself in the interview is absolutely critical to turning in a solid interview performance. There is nothing more devastating to interview success than the inability to successfully navigate this portion of the interview, as the hiring manager begins to hone in on your "weaknesses," "areas for improvement," and "past failures." Throughout the interview, the employer will continue to throw bait into the trap to see if you will take the bait and become ensnared. It will be your challenge to avoid the temptation to take this bait and to artfully steer yourself around the numerous traps that have been set for you along the way.

This does not mean that you are to avoid answering the employer's questions. To do so will surely cause your candidacy to go under. Instead, you need to develop some advance strategies that will allow you to give an honest answer to these questions and, at the same time, avoid or minimize the potential damage that could result from ineffective handling of the information that you share.

Sounds like a tall order, doesn't it? Well, it's not as big a deal as you might think. This is especially true if you are familiar with and apply the basic principles of damage control in the interview that I am about to share with you. Take a minute or two to carefully study these principles, since they can frequently do wonders to rescue you from the relentless jaws of employment interview annihilation!

KEY PRINCIPLES OF DAMAGE CONTROL

There are some basic fundamental principles for exercising good damage control in the interview:

- If asked to be self-critical, never pick items that are sure to be fatal to your candidacy (even if true).
- Pick items that are the least damaging.
- Select areas where you have already demonstrated improvement (not areas that continue to be a problem).
- Pick traits and characteristics that could also be seen as positives.
- Never make an "absolute" negative statement about yourself.
- Don't ever apologize for (or over explain) shortcomings.
- Don't dwell on negatives—be direct, to the point, and then move the conversation to your counterbalancing strengths and assets.
- Always hang a "positive anchor" on any negative statement you make about yourself.
- Cite "contrary evidence" that suggests others have not seen this as a problem.
- Keep things in context—showing that although a "minor" issue the shortcoming has not proven a "major" problem in getting the job done.
- Volunteer that you can provide names of others who can confirm your assessment that the "weakness" was not a major problem in the context of your overall performance.

Let's now examine these principles so that you thoroughly understand them and can become skilled at applying them in improving your overall interview effectiveness.

Picking Nonfatal Items

No matter what the topical area, when asked to be critical of yourself and to cite "opportunities for improvement" during the course of the interview, never volunteer the worst possible thing you can say about yourself. Whether discussing your technical competence, your motivation, your past work environment, your relationship with your boss, your interpersonal relationships, or past failures—whatever the topic—avoid choosing the "worst case scenario." Especially, don't volunteer negative information that could prove severely damaging or even fatal to your employment candidacy.

Don't try to avoid answering the question or beating around the bush. You are being asked a serious question and it deserves a serious answer. Being obtuse or evasive is not going to make a favorable impression on the employer and is sure to backfire. Instead, be open, direct, straightforward, and to the point. Answer the question, but, by all means, be "commercial" in your answer.

Pick "weaknesses" or "areas for improvement" that are the least damaging to your candidacy. Where possible, select areas that, although you may be somewhat vulnerable, you have been able to demonstrate reasonable improvement. Tell the employer what you have done to improve in these areas and the results you have gotten from your efforts. Demonstrate that you are a person who is willing to take responsibility for your shortcomings, but who is also willing and motivated to improve yourself.

The following short scenario should help cement these points:

Example 1

Employer: *What can you cite as a key area for personal improvement in your overall job performance?*

Candidate: *Well, quite frankly, Jim, I feel my performance has been quite good. And, I think my boss would agree. However, I sometimes have a tendency to be a little more detailed than perhaps I should. Although not a major issue, I've forced myself to be more attentive in this area, and know that I have improved. In fact my boss, Mary*

Johnson, commented favorably about this during my last performance evaluation.

Example 2

Employer: *What aspect of your performance could you most improve?*

Candidate: *Well, generally my performance would be seen as very good. However, if I were forced to select an area for improvement, I suppose I would say that I have a tendency to sometimes be a little more intense than I should. Perhaps I should occasionally kick back a little and be a little more relaxed in my approach to my work. I tend to be somewhat more task-focused and results-oriented than most, making me seem more serious than I really am.*

In most quarters, being "detail-oriented," "task-focused," and "somewhat intense" would not be seen as particularly injurious to a person's employment candidacy since, as described here, it is clear that these attributes have certainly had minimal consequence from a job performance standpoint. Certainly, for most employers, such attributes would hardly be seen as "show stoppers," and are good examples of the kind of benign self-criticism that will likely cause little or no concern on the employer's part.

Negatives That Are Also Positives

Many traits and characteristics that are seen as negatives, when viewed slightly differently, can also be seen as positives. It depends on which lens you are looking through.

For example, being detailed (a potential negative) can also mean being thorough (a positive). Likewise, someone who is seen as fussy might also be described as neat and meticulous. Someone who is cautious may also be seen as careful, fastidious, or safety conscious. A less cautious, hipshooter type might also be seen as risk-taking, entrepreneurial, or results-driven. Yes, beauty is clearly in the eye of the beholder, and simply shifting the adjectives used to describe yourself can cause a reverse shift in the paradigm from negative to positive.

For example, when asked by the interviewer to talk about improvement areas in your workstyle, you will want to pick self-descriptors that can be seen as both a positive and a negative. And, you will want to shift the paradigm to demonstrate that these negatives can also prove to be one of your key strengths—something that has potential positive impact for the employer. Take time also to point out to the interviewer how this might also prove beneficial should you be hired.

No "Absolute" Negative Statements

When answering difficult questions requiring self-criticism, remember not to be too tough on yourself. Never make an "absolute" negative statement about yourself. Always leave some room for doubt that this particular descriptor totally applies to you.

For example, never say, "I am too lenient with the people I manage." This is an absolute negative statement. Instead say something like,

Sometimes I may have a tendency to be a little more lenient with subordinates than I should. I feel that it is important, however, to give the people who work for me a certain amount of freedom in determining how to do their work. This keeps them challenged and motivated. Sometimes it is a fine line between being too controlling or too lenient. On the other hand, if you reel people in too fast or keep them on too tight a leash, they may lose their energy and enthusiasm for their work. It's a very fine line to tread.

In this example, you can see how the candidate did not attempt to evade the issue. The interview question was honestly answered, and the candidate willingly volunteered an area for improvement. Use of the word "sometimes" is an effective technique for avoiding making an absolute negative statement. If you make an absolute statement by saying that you *are too lenient with people,"* the interviewer will take you at your word, attaching the tag *"too lenient with people"* to your candidacy. On the other hand, by saying that "sometimes" you may have a tendency to be too lenient, you avoid this absolute negative tag. This suggests that you are not always this way, and in fact implies that there are times when you certainly are not too lenient in dealing with others. All of this is captured by simply prefixing or qualifying the statement with use of the word "sometimes."

Also note use of the words "may have a tendency." As with the word "sometimes," these words suggest that you have a leaning in a certain direction but that you are able to strike a reasonable balance since it is not an "absolute" state of being.

In other words, saying that you *"may have a tendency"* to be too lenient suggests that you also have some flexibility and balance in your style. The message taken away by the interviewer is that this may be the tendency (i.e., too lenient), but there are times when you will likely "get tough" as well. This more balanced view tends to qualify and neutralize the negative message gotten from making an absolute negative statement about yourself (e.g., I am too lenient with people), and will go a long way toward minimizing the damage caused to your employment candidacy.

In my example, you will also want to take note of one other damage control technique that can help your cause. This is to offer a simple *explanation* for your tendency toward what might, in some circumstances, be viewed by the employer as an undesirable tendency or behavior. By *explaining* that you did not wish to stymie subordinate enthusiasm and motivation, you provide a rational, plausible explanation for sometimes being too lenient with others. This suggests to the employer that there is a rational reason for your behavior, and that the net result of your behavior can often have favorable results for the organization.

Whatever you do, however, avoid the inclination to over-explain your reasons for this "negative" behavior. To do so will make you appear overly defensive in the eyes of the employer, which will tend to suggest that this is far more of a problem than you might like to admit. So, keep your explanation plausible, brief, and move on to the next topic.

Hang a Positive Anchor

Another key principle for effectively managing negative information in the employment interview is to always hang a positive anchor on any negative statement that you make about yourself. Doing so will tend to neutralize the impression left by the negative information shared with the employer. This is a pretty powerful technique for achieving a high level of damage control in the interview.

Much of what might be perceived as negative attributes about a person, if turned a slightly different way, can also be seen as positives. This has to do with shifting the paradigm, or changing the way the interviewer thinks about these attributes by suggesting in what ways these same attributes might also prove beneficial.

At Brandywine Consulting Group (my outplacement consulting firm), we have experimented with this phenomenon while working with groups of outplaced employees recently separated from their employers. During interview training, we play a game with the group called "Shifting the Paradigm." In this game, we ask each person in the group to name one or two negative things they could say about themselves if forced to be self-critical in an employment interview. We then ask the group to take these negative attributes and to think of different ways to say the same thing so that these attributes might also be seen by the employer as a positive. Interestingly, we have yet to fail to make the conversion from negative to positive. The following partial listing of paired negative attributes and their corresponding positive descriptions should help make this point more clearly:

Negative Trait	*Positive Attribute*
1. overly detailed	1. thorough, reliable
2. cautious	2. careful, accurate
3. intense	3. focused, motivated
4. disorganized	4. creative, free-thinking

Negative Trait	*Positive Attribute*
5. slow	5. methodical, careful
6. impersonal	6. focused, goal-oriented
7. argumentative	7. principled, confident
8. controlling	8. results-oriented
9. stubborn	9. dedicated, persistent
10. insensitive	10. direct, straightforward
11. naive	11. open, honest
12. confrontive	12. nonpolitical, principled
13. pragmatic	13. practical, utilitarian
14. vague	14. strategic, noncontrolling
15. aggressive	15. assertive, persistent

By choosing slightly different words to describe the same attribute, you can change what may first appear to be a negative trait into a positive attribute. It's all in what words you choose and how you choose to use them to describe yourself to the interviewer.

In the paired list, the "positive attributes" become the positive anchors you hang onto the "negative traits" you are forced to share with the employer. By pairing these negative traits with their corresponding positive attributes, you can pretty much neutralize the negative information shared with the employer, by shifting the employer's paradigm and focus from the negative to the positive.

Here are some examples of how this might be done:

Example 1

Employer: *If you were to ask your colleagues what you could do to improve yourself, what do you think they would say?*

Candidate: *Well, some might say that sometimes I may have a tendency to be somewhat stubborn, and need to be a little more flexible. However, on the other hand, they would also probably agree that I am straightforward, very principled, and can be completely trusted as well.*

Example 2

Employer: *If I asked your boss in what area you could most improve, what do you feel he would choose?*

Candidate: *He would most likely say that I sometimes have a tendency to be overly detailed. But, he would also probably tell you that I am very thorough and can be totally relied upon to get things done with a high degree of accuracy.*

Example 3

Employer: *What aspect of your overall performance could most be improved?*

Candidate: *Perhaps, at times, I could be more tolerant of others' work styles and levels of commitment to the business. I tend to be very hard-working and results-driven, and am not always as tolerant of others who are less committed to business goals. However, I think most would also tell you that I have a very positive, motivational influence on others, and am someone they value as a team member.*

These examples should clearly demonstrate how hanging a positive anchor on an initial negative statement can tend to neutralize the effect of the negative factor. Describing the negative trait and tagging on the corresponding positive attributes can prove a powerful way to control the damage caused by sharing a negative self-criticism in the interview discussion. In fact, in many cases, hanging on such a "positive anchor" can sometimes totally flip the initial negative image to a very favorable impression.

Keep Things in Context

When sharing negative or potentially damaging information about yourself in the interview, be sure to describe the negative in the context of your "total" or "overall" job performance. If you let it stand alone, it is sure to stick out as a problem in the mind of the employer. Framing it in the context of your overall job performance, however, can often reduce its negative impact on the interviewer and cause the employer to have a more "balanced" view of your performance (and thus a more favorable impression of your candidacy).

This is why it is important, when asked to describe areas for performance improvement, that you begin your response by first stating that you believe your overall job performance to be quite good, and then follow this by describing the improvement area. By doing this, you are casting this improvement need in the context of your overall performance which guards against it from becoming "larger than life" from the employer's perspective. Most employers understand that there are always areas for some kind of improvement in one's job performance. We are simply trying to keep things from getting blown out of proportion.

The following are some examples of approaches you might use to frame your answers in the context of total job performance:

Example 1

Employer: *What aspect of your performance could you most improve?*

Candidate: *I think most would tell you that my performance is quite good. However, I guess there is always some room for improvement. I suppose if I had to choose an improvement area it would be to improve my knowledge of re-engineering techniques. Although I certainly understand the basics, I would like to take an advanced workshop in re-engineering. I have had this on my "to do" list for the last six months or so, but my work schedule has not afforded me the time to do it.*

Example 2

Employer: *What do you consider to be your single greatest weakness—the thing that, if you did something about it, would most allow you to improve your effectiveness?*

Candidate: *Although generally most would perceive my performance to be very strong, I suppose I could be a little less intense in my work style. I sometimes get so focused on the mission that I believe others are working as rapidly as I am, only to find that they are not nearly as far along. I suppose I need to be a little more relaxed in my approach. This has certainly never really been a major issue, however, and I generally tend to get along well with others.*

Example 3

Employer: *What do you consider to be your biggest failure in your career to-date?*

Candidate: *I can honestly say that I don't believe I've ever had a real failure. My performance has always be rated better than average. Perhaps my biggest personal disappointment, however, was my job with Kennsington Corporation. I was disappointed that the job didn't provide for more exposure to manufacturing operations than it did. I suppose I could have done a better job of determining this during the job interview. As a result, the job wasn't quite as stimulating as I had hoped. In this sense, I suppose it would rank as my biggest career failure to-date. However, despite my disappointment, I worked hard at the job and performed my job responsibilities well.*

As you can see from these examples, framing the personal improvement area in the context of your overall job performance, and stating that it has not had a significant impact on job performance, can certainly deflate the potentially negative impact of sharing this kind of self-critical information with the employer.

Don't Dwell on Negatives

One mistake often made by inexperienced interviewees is to dwell too long on negative information. There is sometimes the tendency to overexplain. Avoid this tendency. Don't over explain or apologize for personal or technical shortcomings. To do so can suggest to the employer that things were a greater issue than they really were.

When responding to interview questions that require you to offer self-criticism or identify areas for personal improvement, be brief, to the point and, at your first opportunity, transition focus to your positive attributes that suggest that you are a viable candidate for the opening. Droning on and on about your shortcomings will suggest to the interviewer that you are being overly defensive and thus probably have something to hide. Why otherwise would you spend so much time explaining this point?

As we have seen in our previous examples, hanging positive anchors on negative statements that you have made about yourself is probably the most effective way to quickly transition the employer's focus from this potential negative to your strengths and positive attributes. Intentionally using this positive anchor strategy will also force you to be brief and to-the-point, not allowing time for offering too much explanation.

Being able to openly describe a shortcoming and then gracefully transition to your positive attributes also suggests to the employer that you are psychologically sound. It demonstrates that you have a balanced view of your personal make-up, and do not overly dwell on your deficits. Conversely, over explaining a shortcoming can suggest that you lack such a well-balanced perspective about yourself, and that you feel a need to engage in less rational, defensive behavior.

So, when discussing negative information, be brief, matter-of-fact, to-the-point, non-apologetic, and return the conversation to discussion of your positive attributes at the earliest, reasonable opportunity. Avoid indulging in self-deprecation, at all costs!

Citing Contrary Evidence

From a damage control standpoint, one of the most difficult situations to manage in the employment interview is having to disclose that you were evaluated as a "poor performer" by a current or former boss, or that you and your boss simply did not get along. Disclosure of this kind of information is bound to send shivers up an employer's spine and cause great concern about your overall suitability for employment. How you manage these topics will certainly have major impact on interview results, and is therefore worthy of some careful planning on your part.

As the former human resources manager for the corporate staff of a major Fortune 200 company, I have had a lot of experience dealing with poor performance issues. I have counseled and advised numerous managers and executives as they consciously worked to lay the ground work for performance-based terminations of subordinates with whom they were unhappy.

From firsthand observation, as well as from discussions with several other human resources managers on this subject, I can tell you that most performance issues truly have little to do with technical competence (i.e., the ability of the individual to perform the technical aspects of the job). Instead, an extremely high percentage of performance issues (estimated at 90% or better) have to do with the lack of fit with the organization's culture.

Since organizational culture is most often heavily defined by the individual philosophy, style, and values of the functional manager who leads the immediate work group, this usually means that "poor performers" are those individuals who are simply not compatible with the boss. Poor performers are invariably those persons who do not exhibit the preferred characteristics, traits, style, and behaviors valued and favored by the boss. Failure to align with the boss's preferred behaviors and core value system, almost without exception, eventually spells performance disaster.

Although these "poor performers" can be technically competent, since they think differently from the boss and do not share the boss's values, they are viewed as "not fitting in." As this incompatibility becomes increasingly apparent, words that begin to be used by the boss in describing such persons are: uncooperative, argumentive, poor interpersonal skills, incompatible with the group, a loner, doesn't understand the priorities, not supportive of our goals, lacks motivation, insubordinate, and so on.

Despite the fact that these persons may be quite competent technically, not sharing the same philosophy and value system with the boss will almost guarantee performance failure. The subordinate will generally experience great difficulty in getting support for his or her ideas, and the resources necessary for performance success. Under these circumstances, poor performance seems ordained from the beginning, regardless of the employee's overall capability. It is the inevitable outcome of such a relationship.

Regardless of its genesis, poor performance is a difficult topic to handle in the context of the employment interview. How does one handle strong differences with the boss from an interview standpoint? What is the best way to present this kind of information to the prospective employer without totally annihilating your employment prospects? This is an exceedingly difficult interview challenge for most candidates to handle, and requires a carefully thought-out strategy for doing so.

I believe the best way to manage this kind of an issue is to hit it head on. Although you may wish to downplay the severity of the problem somewhat and choose just the right words in describing it, there is no point in denying that a problem exists. Chances are that the employer is going to uncover this problem during the course of conducting a reference check. If the employer is not conditioned in advance to expect this kind of information, such negative information would come as a complete surprise and cause the employer to have serious reservations about your candidacy. Under these circumstances, without the employer having some appropriate forewarning, the employer will most likely become gun shy, and it is highly unlikely that an employment offer will be forthcoming.

If asked about your relationship with your boss or your job performance under these circumstances, you are best advised to be forthcoming and straightforward in your response. Admit that the relationship was less than perfect, but couch your explanation in terms of some differences in basic style or viewpoint. Don't suggest that you were argumentive or combative, only that there was simply an honest difference in your styles and the way you viewed things. Offer this brief explanation of the differences and then provide some historical "contrary evidence," confirming that this particular area has never been a problem for you in the past as you worked for other managers throughout your career.

Here are some examples of how "contrary evidence" might be used to soften the blow:

Example 1

Employer: *If I were to ask your boss about your performance, what would she tell me?*

Candidate: *Well, Mr. Jackson, although she would likely have some good things to say, I'm not sure she would be totally positive about our relationship. Sharon and I have some honest differences in our viewpoints, which is one of the main reasons I have decided to look for a career change. Although Sharon has her strengths as a manager, she also tends to be a controlling style manager who tends to micromanage her subordinates and tell them exactly how they are to do things.*

As a knowledgeable, seasoned professional, quite frankly, I find this kind of close supervision stifling and prefer to work for someone with a more participative management style. Apparently, I am not alone in my feelings since five of our eight department members have resigned in the last six months, and I am aware that one other is looking.

Although, at the appropriate time, you should talk to Sharon, I suggest you also talk to others for whom I have worked in the past. I think you will find unanimous agreement among my past managers, that I have consistently been an excellent worker with whom they enjoyed working.

Example 2

Employer: *How would you describe your relationship with your current boss?*

Candidate: *Well, quite frankly it is not as good as I might like. Although Bill would tell you that he thinks highly of my design engineering and interpersonal skills, if pressed, I think he might also say that he feels that I am sometimes a little slower in getting things done than he would like. We have had some discussion on this point.*

Although conscientious and well-meaning, in my judgment, Bill, as a mechanical engineer, does not have a full understanding and appreciation for some of the intricacies of electronics engineering work. He, therefore, has a tendency to become impatient if he feels things are moving too slowly. Others in group are experiencing the same frustration on this point.

Quite frankly, I've never experienced this kind of situation before. In fact, over the last ten years, I have worked for more than a dozen different functional and project managers, all of whom have been totally satisfied with my performance. I am sure if you talked with them, which I would strongly encourage you to do, they would all be very complimentary of my overall work performance. I have always enjoyed a reputation for being both a productive and quality-conscious worker, and am very conscientious about my performance.

As you can see from these examples, performance issues are a difficult matter to handle effectively in the employment interview. No matter what technique you use and how effectively you address them, there will always be some residue of doubt in the mind of the employer about the suitability of your employment candidacy. The best that you can hope for, under such circumstances, is that they will be objective in their evaluation, and take the time to check the references which you furnish as your "contrary evidence."

Certainly, by providing "contrary evidence" (i.e., others who can vouch for the quality of your performance in the questionable performance area), you stand a chance of offsetting this stumbling block. Also, by couching this issue in an historical perspective (i.e., showing that it has never been an issue in any of your previous jobs), the employer is likely to be more forgiving than if it has been part of a long-term pattern or trend. Citing references who have first-hand knowledge of your work and can confirm your observations on the subject, can also be rather convincing, especially if these references are your past bosses.

Now that I have finished describing the various damage control tactics and techniques that you can use to ward off a direct frontal attack during the course of the job interview, we need to return to more strategic matters. If you are going to substantially improve your odds of winning the interview game, you will need to anticipate the employer's plan of attack and then, using the damage control tactics just learned, develop a solid defensive strategy that will keep your ship afloat under the most withering barrage of enemy firepower.

PREPARING YOUR DEFENSE

Knowing the employer's most probable plan of attack (as previously set forth in this chapter), and applying the damage control principles just discussed, you should now be in a position to take much of the guesswork out of the interview process and begin to prepare an effective defensive strategy. By anticipating much of the employer's probable line-of-inquiry (which we have done earlier), and preparing an appropriate response, you are far less vulnerable than if you simply go into the interview leaving things to chance. In such a case, you are totally and completely at the mercy of the employer.

The best way to plan your defensive strategy is to systematically address each of the six key areas most likely to be probed by the employer in advance of your interview. This should be done with a view toward determining where you are most vulnerable, and to decide in advance what will be the most effective evasive strategy for you to deploy. The following process, along with related planning forms, should help you to effectively accomplish this task.

As you prepare your interview strategy for each of these six areas, be sure to use damage control principles and techniques to control and minimize the potential damage that could result from sharing negative information with the employer.

Technical Competence

- With what aspects of the job are you least comfortable from a performance standpoint? Why?
- What specific knowledge, skill, or experience do you lack that accounts for this discomfort?
- How badly does this deficit hamper your performance? Is it serious?
- Have these items been discussed during past performance evaluations?
- What was said about their impact on your performance?
- How have you compensated for these in the past?
- What have you done to offset these deficits?
- What have you done (are you doing) to improve your capability in these areas, and with what success?

- How are you going to handle this in the interview?
- Using damage control techniques, how will you describe this deficit in a way that will be least damaging to your employment candidacy?
- What strengths do you have that more than offset this shortcoming?

List below those technical weaknesses you plan to share with the employer. (*Hint:* Pick the two or three that will be least damaging and are least critical to successful job performance. Select those where you can demonstrate some improvement. List the least damaging first, second least damaging second, etc.)

_____

_____

_____

_____

How will you describe these weaknesses to the employer? (*Hint:* Apply the damage control principles listed on pages 36 to 39.)

_____

_____

_____

_____

_____

_____

_____

Job Motivation

- Of the past jobs you have held, which did you least enjoy?
- What aspects of these jobs did you find most satisfying?
- What aspects did you find least satisfying?
- Why did these job aspects prove less stimulating or motivational?
- What specifically caused your dissatisfaction?
- Based upon past jobs that you found particularly satisfying, what was missing from these less satisfying jobs?

When asked in the interview, what past jobs will you describe as being least satisfying? (*Hint:* Pick jobs least similar to the jobs for which you will be interviewing. It is especially helpful to select jobs that were routine, did not offer much challenge, and did not utilize your full potential.)

_____

_____

_____

What will you describe as being the factors that accounted for your dissatisfaction? (*Hint:* Pick factors less likely to be present in the job or work environment for which you are interviewing. Select factors that are least critical to overall job performance of the position. Keep things in context, stating that although dissatisfying, these factors did not significantly impact your overall job performance.)

_____

_____

_____

_____

What reasons will you state for your dissatisfaction? (*Hint:* Choose reasons that don't relate to the position for which you are being interviewed and would have little influence on performance of the new position.)

_____

_____

_____

_____

_____

_____

Fit with Work Environment

- In which past work environment(s) were you least happy?
- What factors most influenced your negative feeling?
- What impact did these have on you? What did you do?
- How serious was the situation, and how did you cope?
- How did this impact your overall job performance?
- What actions did you take to overcome this obstacle?
- What factors need to be present (or absent) in the work environment to ensure your happiness?

Which past work environment will you cite as least satisfying if asked in the interview? (*Hint:* Pick one that is most dissimilar from the new work environment in which you would be working.)

_____

_____

_____

What factors will you cite in the interview that contributed to your dissatisfaction? (*Hint:* Pick factors that are least likely to be a problem in the new work environment. Select factors with which you could cope, and which have little or no impact on your work performance.)

_____

_____

_____

_____

_____

_____

How will you describe the impact these factors had on your productivity and overall effectiveness? (*Hint:* Describe what you did to cope, and why these factors had little or no impact on your overall performance.)

_____

_____

_____

_____

_____

_____

_____

Fit with Boss

- With which past boss(es) did you least enjoy working?
- What did the boss do (not do) that caused your dissatisfaction?
- What characteristics of this boss(es) caused you discomfort (i.e., philosophy, personal style, management style, traits, characteristics, behaviors, etc.)?
- How did you respond to these?
- What impact did this have on your overall performance?
- What did you do to best manage this relationship?
- What were the results of your efforts?

How will you describe your least-liked boss? What adjectives will you use to describe this person's characteristics? (*Hint:* Avoid describing someone with the same characteristics as the new boss with whom you are interviewing. Unless untrue, state that you have had a good relationship with all of your past bosses, and that you did not really dislike the boss that you have chosen to describe. You have simply liked working for him or her less than others for whom you have worked.)

_____

_____

_____

_____

_____

_____

What will you say when asked in the interview what impact this boss had on you? (*Hint:* State that this boss had little or no impact on your overall job performance, and that you continued to turn in good performance despite these minor frustrations.)

_____

_____

_____

_____

_____

What will you tell the employer about how you managed this relationship, and what results were realized from your efforts? (*Hint:* Cite positive examples of things you did to improve this relationship, especially where they were successful. Describe these successes. Avoid describing failed attempts to improve the relationship. Emphasize again that despite these minor issues, you had a generally positive relationship.)

_____

_____

_____

_____

_____

_____

_____

Interpersonal Relationships

- With what kind of people do you least get along?
- What is there about such people that causes you to feel this way?
- What do such individuals have in common?
- How are they different from those with whom you enjoy working?
- What do they do (or not do) to make you dislike them?
- What impact has this had on you? What do you do?
- How do you cope with such people?
- What have you done to improve these relationships?
- What have been the results of these efforts?
- What successes have you had?

How will you describe the characteristics of people with whom you most dislike working? (*Hint:* Pick persons least like the group with whom you are interviewing. Select persons with whom you were successful in patching things up, and describe their characteristics. Avoid using your worst enemy as the prototype, the one with whom you have never gotten along no matter what you've done.)

_____

_____

_____

_____

What will you say when asked to describe how you have managed these kinds of relationships—what have you done and how did it work? (*Hint:* You don't want to appear that you have had a history of interpersonal problems. Put things in context. Tell them that you get along with just about everybody, so interpersonal skills have not been a problem for you. Cite one or two persons with whom you had an issue, but were able to patch things up. Describe what you did, and the favorable results achieved.)

_____

_____

_____

_____

_____

_____

_____

_____

Past Failures

- What has been your single biggest job-related disappointment or failure?
- What factors most accounted for this disappointment or failure?
- If more than one failure or major disappointment, has there been a pattern to these?
- What has that pattern been?
- What have you learned from these failures or disappointments?

When you are asked in the interview to describe your single biggest job-related disappointment or failure, what will you say? (*Hint:* Pick one that is least related to the type of job for which you are interviewing—one that is least likely to suggest that you will have a performance problem with this position. Stick more with disappointments, where you misjudged things, rather than an out-and-out performance failure.)

_____

_____

_____

What will you describe as the key factors that accounted for this failure or disappointment? (*Hint:* Choose factors that have little bearing on performance of the position for which you are interviewing.)

_____

_____

_____

_____

_____

_____

_____

If you have done your work well, you are now extremely well-prepared to handle a high percentage of the negative questions that are likely to come your way during the typical employment interview. By thinking your way through these in advance, and using good damage control techniques, you will probably be very successful at effectively fielding these tough questions with little or no negative impact on your interview results.

ADVANCE INTELLIGENCE

No chapter on damage control in the interview would be complete without at least a brief mention of the importance of advance intelligence. Without some advance idea of the kinds of answers the employer will find desirable or acceptable, it will be pretty hard to initiate an effective damage control strategy.

For example, one employer may feel it is desirable to have persons who are aggressive, strong-willed, decisive, risk-taking, and so on. Another employer may view these same attributes as undesirable and instead prefer candidates who are assertive, open to other ideas, flexible, a team player, and so on. These are two distinctly different profiles.

In the case of the first company, citing criticism of a former boss who stated that you were too aggressive, inflexible, too quick to act might not be very damaging to interview results. In fact, it is possible that this company might even view these as positive attributes. Providing the same information to the second company, however, would be quite a different story.

What is viewed as positive attributes by one employer may well be viewed as negative by another. What you are preparing in advance as your best defensive strategy for interview damage control, therefore, could potentially backfire without some specific advance information about the culture of the organization and management style of the hiring manager with whom you will be interviewing.

Unless you have some close ties with others in the department or work group in which you would be employed, it is next to impossible to get much if any advanced intelligence on these topics. If, on the other hand, you are friendly with some of the department members or others who work closely with the hiring manager with whom you will be interviewing, with a little work it might be quite possible to get some advance intelligence which could prove extremely helpful to formulating an effective interview strategy.

In the event you have such pre-existing relationships, a quick survey of these individuals using the following set of questions will provide some exceptionally useful information which can serve to provide you with a real leg up in preparing you for the interview. Here is how you might handle such questions:

Hi, Joan, this is Dave Smith calling. How have you been? Listen, Joan, I will be coming in to Fulton Company on Friday to interview with Sandra Wilkinson for a position as Senior Buyer. I was wondering if you would be willing to share some observations about what kind of a person Sandra is, what it might be like to work for her, and what the general work environment is like in the Procurement group?

After this or a similar introduction, here are some key questions that should help to pry loose some very helpful information and insight:

1. How would you categorize Sandra Wilkinson as a manager?
2. What observation can you make about her management style and philosophy?
3. How would you describe her personal style—her traits, characteristics, behaviors?
4. What do you think she is like to work for?
5. Can you make some observations about the work environment in the Procurement Department?
6. What is it like to work there?
7. From what you know about Sandra, what do you feel is going to be important to be viewed as a strong player by her?
8. As you think about what are viewed by her as high performers within the Procurement function, what seems characteristic or unique about this group?
9. What kinds of employees does she appear less supportive of?
10. What do you feel will be important to do in the interview to create a favorable impression with Sandra?
11. Is there any other advice you have for me?

Answers to these, and similar questions, will arm you with some excellent information that should prove extremely useful in formulating a winning interview strategy. Not only will it tell you what areas to emphasize in the interview, but it will also provide some strong clues about how to best handle information that the hiring manager might view as less than favorable. Certainly it will provide you with key information that will be helpful in fine-tuning your defensive strategy, to assure that you present yourself in the most favorable light.

In the absence of personal contacts who can provide you with inside information about your future boss and work environment, advance intelligence is much harder to come by. In such cases, you are going to have to rely on your interviewing skills to provide you with as much of this information as you can get early in the interview discussion. In absence of this information, you will be pretty much shooting in the dark.

Provided the circumstances allow you to do it and provided you are interviewing with someone who is not an interview control freak, you might be lucky enough to get off a couple of key questions that should prove helpful to formulating the rest of your interview strategy. To be useful, however, these questions will need to be answered early in the interview discussion.

If interviewing with professional peers who are now working for the same hiring manager (your future boss), you might try a few of the following questions:

1. What is it like to work for Michael?
2. How would you describe his management style?
3. As a manager, what do you consider to be his strong points?
4. In your judgement, what would make him an even better manager?
5. What is the work environment like here?
6. How does it compare with other places where you have worked?
7. What do you like best?
8. What could be improved?

9. What kinds of people do you feel Michael likes to have working for him?

10. How do you think he might describe a "high performer"?

11. What seems to characterize people of whom he is less supportive?

12. What are the major problems or issues that Michael seems most concerned with?

13. What else can you tell me about working here that would be helpful to know about?

When interviewing directly with the hiring manager (your future boss) you might try some of the same questions, wording them slightly differently. Here are some examples:

1. Michael, from a performance standpoint, what are the things that are most important to you?

2. How would you characterize the high performers in your organization? What sets them apart?

3. How would you categorize those who do not work out well in your organization? What sets them apart from better performers?

4. How would you categorize the work environment in your department? What is it like to work here?

5. How is it different from other environments in which you have worked?

6. What do you feel are the key ingredients for being successful in this position?

7. What do you view as the key challenges of this position?

8. From a goals and objectives standpoint, what do you feel are the important priorities for this position?

As you can readily see, answers to these types of questions will provide you with enormous insight into what the hiring manager feels is particularly important in a successful candidate. From a damage control standpoint, it will also provide you with some excellent advance intelligence (especially if answered early in the discussion) to alert you to some important shifts or modifications in your defensive strategy that will allow you to more effectively manage potentially damaging information that could prove fatal to your employment candidacy.

Hopefully, this chapter has armed you with the strategies and techniques that will keep your ship afloat through the toughest part of the interview battle and provide you with what you need to get you safely into port. Some careful advance preparation can go a long way toward making this happen.

5

INTERVIEW QUESTIONS— STRENGTHS

KEY INTERVIEW QUESTIONS

Interview questions directed at your "strengths" (both technical and personal) can be asked in several different ways. The following variations should prove to be an excellent warm-up exercise for preparing you to address this important interview category:

- *What do you consider your greatest strengths or assets?*
- *What factors most account for your career success to-date?*
- *What do you consider your most outstanding qualities?*
- *In what areas are others most complimentary of you?*
- *During performance reviews, what areas have most frequently been cited as your key strengths?*

- *From a job performance standpoint, what do you consider to be your major attributes?*
- *In checking with your co-workers, in what areas would they describe you as most effective?*
- *What aspects of this position do you feel you will perform particularly well?*
- *Describe your three greatest strengths and tell me how you have used these to realize improvements in your current job.*
- *Which two or three major accomplishments best illustrate your key strengths?*
- *In what ways do you consider your qualifications unique or distinctive from others applying for this position?*
- *Why should I hire you for this position?*
- *What do your co-workers most admire or value about you?*
- *If asked, what would your current boss cite as your three greatest strengths or attributes?*
- *When compared with other department members, in what areas do you most excel?*
- *In what areas do others most rely or depend upon you?*
- *What would a thorough reference check reveal as your strongest attributes?*
- *In what aspects of your current job have you most excelled?*
- *On a scale of 1 to 10 (10 being high), which of your overall qualifications would you rate at the "9" or "10" level?*
- *What single skill or capability has most contributed to your career success?*
- *Why should we choose you over other candidates for this position?*

It is unimaginable to think that an employment interview would ever take place without the candidate being asked, in one form or another, to describe his or her key strengths.

You can pretty much bet the ranch that this question will be the focal point of much interest and attention during the course of your employment interviews. How well this question is answered is sure to have a major impact on the outcome of your employment interview.

An individual candidate's strengths or key capabilities is at the very heart of the interview and selection process. When interviewing, the employer already has in mind certain qualifications that are felt to be important to successful performance of the position. A key objective of the interview from the employer's perspective, therefore, becomes to determine whether the candidate's strengths or key competencies align well with these predetermined qualifications. If the candidate's strengths are in those areas thought to be important to successful job performance, interest in the candidate is bound to be high. Conversely, if the person's key strengths are in areas thought to be unrelated to successful performance of the position, the employer is bound to move on in search of "better qualified" candidates.

INTERVIEW STRATEGY

Successful interview strategy in addressing this category requires some careful thought and practice prior to arriving for the interview. Unless you are awfully good at thinking quickly on your feet, you will be leaving a lot to chance in not giving careful thought how best to address this area in advance of the interview meeting. In fact, there is a high likelihood that such lack of preparation could well cost you a good job offer.

Careful analysis of the sample questions just cited shows that there are three distinct components to the "key strengths" question. These are:

1. Identification of key strengths (as described by self or others).

2. Evidence of key strength utilization (as demonstrated in major contributions, job success, career success).

3. Comparison with peers (co-workers, other applicants for position).

You should be thinking in these terms as you determine which particular strengths you will want to emphasize during the interview.

A good strategy to use when addressing this issue is to pretend that you are the employer, and try to determine what specific skills and capabilities are going to be most important to successful job performance. The following set of questions should prove helpful in ferreting out this information:

- What are the key responsibilities of the position?
- What are the key results expected in each of these responsibility areas?
- What major problems must be solved (or challenges met) in order to achieve these results?
- What important skills or capabilities are needed to successfully solve these major problems and achieve the desired functional results?
- What key strengths does this suggest a candidate must have in order to be successful in the position?
- Which of these are among my strongest attributes?

Answering the above questions should provide you with some excellent clues about the key strengths and capabilities that will likely be sought by the employer in filling the targeted position. You are going to need to be prepared to cite these as key strength areas if you expect to generate much, if any, interest in your candidacy.

The logic of this approach to advance interview preparation is impeccable. It is estimated that employers commit better than 70 percent of the average interview to examining and evaluating the candidate's "technical qualifications," that is, his or her specialized knowledge and ability to solve key problems and achieve the desired results the organization is seeking in key areas of job accountability. Being skilled at articulating "key strengths" in these important performance-related areas is critical to making a good showing in the employment interview.

With today's heavy reliance on behavioral-based interviewing techniques by employers, being able to simply cite these strengths in most job interviews will not be enough. The majority of employers are going to want to see "evidence" of your ability to apply these strengths in achieving actual results. You will therefore need to be prepared to cite specific major improvements and key accomplishments that were realized by your employer(s) as a result of your application of these "strengths" in solving important problems and meeting the special challenges of your current and past positions.

Good interview performance will require you to be able to link your strengths with major accomplishments. Perhaps a good way to prepare for this, as part of your advance interview preparation, would be to reverse the process and start with key accomplishments first. You may find the following approach helpful in accomplishing this analysis:

- For each position you have held, identify three to four major accomplishments or improvements you brought about.

- If you are having trouble answering this, think about what problems existed when you first came into the job, and what you did about them.

- What specific results or benefits were realized by the company as a result of your efforts? (Where possible, describe in quantitative terms to illustrate the degree of improvement realized.)

- What special skills or capabilities allowed you to achieve these results?

- From this analysis, what do you now feel are some of your best job-relevant strengths?

Analysis of a person's strengths normally suggests that these strengths fall into two distinct, but not unrelated categories:

1. Technical strengths.
2. Personal strengths.

Up to this point in time we have been talking about "technical" strengths—the specialized knowledge, skills, and abilities required to solve key problems and perform the job. "Personal" strengths, on the other hand, are those traits and attributes that contribute to your motivation and desire to perform the work particularly well.

These personal strength factors are sometimes referred to as the virtues of good performance. Virtues, in this sense, could be defined as universally desired or valued behavioral traits. Words that come to mind when describing some of these universally desired virtues are open, honest, highly motivated, dedicated, persistent, dedicated, hardworking, persuasive, assertive, loyal, and so on.

Although it is a good idea to have some of these personal virtues "at the ready" for use in describing personal strengths during the interview, you need to work at connecting them with positive, tangible results that the prospective employer would envision as worthwhile. For example, rather than simply saying that you are hardworking, you might want to say that you are known for being hard-working and have "earned a reputation for handling large volumes of work in a relatively short period of time." To further re-enforce the positive benefit to be realized by the employer of your being hard-working, you might want to add something like, "It is for this reason that I am normally the one selected to handle the more difficult, challenging projects." Stressing the benefits of hard-working adds an additional sense of value to your candidacy, because the employer can now see how this will directly benefit his or her organization.

The message here is that you will want to not only make a list of personal strengths and virtues, but you will also want to practice describing how the employer will benefit from these specific strengths. Linkage with benefits is a powerful tool when convincing someone of the value you can bring to their company.

CLASSIC ANSWERS

The following are some classic answers to the interview questions concerning your major strengths that should prove helpful to you in formulating your own responses to this particular interview set:

My three major strengths are that I am creative, results-oriented, and continuous-improvement driven. My whole approach to work has been one where I purposely review how work is being done to look for those improvement opportunities that will have the greatest impact. Identifying the major barriers to improvement in these areas, I look for creative ways to eliminate these barriers and move on to bring the improvement about.

For example, in the employment area, cost-per-hire had become an issue. Basic analysis of the problem showed that we were interviewing seven candidates for every offer made—far too many. To address this, I initiated a phone screening process combined with some basic training in phone interviewing techniques. Through better screening, we reduced the interview-to-offer ratio by 50 percent with a resultant 25 percent reduction in hiring costs. This saved the company about $ 0.5 million in employment costs last year alone.

I am always looking for opportunities to become more efficient and save money and time for the company.

* * *

My co-workers would likely tell you that my strongest attributes are persistence and determination. I have developed a reputation for being determined and persistant in tackling difficult problems. I am not a person who gives up easily.

The best example I can give you was the Briar account. We were bidding on a $4 million contract for office furniture, and my company had been told that Briar had decided to give the business to our competitor. Learning this, I immediately called the buyer and told her that the Briar account was extremely important to us and we couldn't afford to lose their business. I asked her what it would take to earn her business back. The answer was "better service." I then asked what kind of service improvement would be most beneficial, and she *replied,"Guaranteed delivery within 30 days of the order." I asked her if we could provide such a guarantee, would she consider awarding the contract to us? She said "yes."*

My persistence paid off. We not only got the original $4 million contract, but have done another $10 million business with Briar in the last six months alone.

* * *

The strength that most sets me apart from others in my department is my technical knowledge of physical testing. I used experimental design techniques to simulate ten-year wear on conveyor bearings, reducing new product testing time by nearly 80 percent. This has enabled us to more than double the new product output and gets us to market with these new products much faster than our competitors.

* * *

Yes, if I were you, I would give serious consideration to hiring me over other candidates you may be considering. One of my key strengths is cost cutting. You already told me that you need to get your manufacturing costs down by at least 25 percent in order to compete with the Detroit plant for the Ford business.

Cost cutting is one of my areas of strength. While working as a manufacturing engineer for New Departure, for example, I brought about improvement to the brake manufacturing line that cut brake manufacturing costs by 30 percent over two years. Finding creative ways to cut costs is a definite strong point, and I feel confident that, with some careful analysis, I can help you achieve your cost-cutting objectives as well.

As you can see from these examples, linking key strengths with actual results can be a powerful interviewing technique that enhances your value and desirability as an employment candidate. It is certainly far more convincing than simply providing a laundry list of your key assets.

6

INTERVIEW QUESTIONS— WEAKNESSES

KEY INTERVIEW QUESTIONS

More interviews are lost by candidates due to their inability to effectively answer questions concerning their major weaknesses (sometimes described as "areas for improvement") than any other area of the employment interview. Sometimes the "weaknesses" area is well-disguised by the employer by virtue of the form the question takes, nonetheless, the questions are the same.

Here are several ways the employer may elect to ask you about your shortcomings:

- *What do you feel are your major weaknesses?*
- *What has been your single most significant work-related failure to-date? Why?*

- *All of us have areas in which we could improve our overall performance. What are some areas in which you could improve?*
- *From a work-related standpoint, what is your biggest shortcoming and why?*
- *What areas has your boss suggested for your improvement?*
- *As you view your qualifications for this position, what do you feel might be some of your development needs?*
- *What would you most like to improve about yourself, and why?*
- *What steps have you taken to improve your overall performance, and why?*
- *What self-improvements could you make that would enhance your overall value to a company?*
- *During a reference check, what areas will likely be suggested by others as areas for your improvement?*
- *During past performance reviews, what areas have been identified for improvement?*
- *In what ways could you improve your overall job performance?*
- *In what ways could you improve your effectiveness with others?*
- *What would you cite as the three areas of your performance that could most be improved?*
- *What aspects of your current position could be better performed, and what improvement is most needed?*
- *If we asked two or three of your co-workers to identify the three areas in which you could most improve, what would they choose?*
- *If you could, what two or three things would you most like to change about yourself to improve your work effectiveness, and why?*
- *What steps have you taken during the last year to improve your overall performance?*

- *In what ways could you improve your interpersonal effectiveness?*
- *How could you most improve your overall capability?*
- *What factors have most stood in the way of your career success to-date?*

Success in the interview is determined not just by how well you present your key strengths and assets, but by how well you handle the "negative" side of the equation as well. Employers will do their best to ferret out your weaknesses and improvement needs as a key item in their decision-making process. Some estimate that "negative" questions, such as those cited here, will likely comprise as much as 25 percent of the interview.

You will see a fair sprinkling of this type of interview question in the great majority of employment interviews that you experience. Learning how to successfully field these kinds of questions will clearly have major impact on your interview success. This area, above all others, is the "leading killer" of most would-be employment candidates. It is estimated that better than 75 percent of all interview "deaths" are caused by the inability to field these kinds of questions—a good reason for you to be well-prepared.

INTERVIEW STRATEGY

Close examination of the sample questions will reveal that there are three main target areas for probing your shortcomings in the employment interview. These are:

1. Technical shortcomings (i.e., the knowledge and skills required to perform the job).
2. Interpersonal shortcomings (i.e., your ability to relate to others in the performance of your job).
3. Personal shortcomings (i.e., your personal traits, characteristics, and behaviors that influence your effectiveness).

In preparing to answer this set of interview questions, I recommend that you identify two to three improvement areas for each of these three target areas. In most cases, a good interviewer will not let you get away by citing only one improvement area. You can likely count on being asked for two or three.

When formulating your response, you will find the following guidelines helpful in minimizing the damage that can result from improper or inept response to this important interview area:

- Choose shortcomings that are not severe, and will likely prove least damaging to your candidacy.
- Pick those weaknesses that are least-related to performance of key aspects of the job.
- Select areas where you have already experienced improvement, demonstrating your willingness and motivation to improve.
- Pick weaknesses that, if viewed differently, may also be seen as strengths (e.g., being "too detailed" could also be seen as "thorough" or "accurate," "stubbornness" could also be seen as "persistence" or "principled").
- Avoid stating your weaknesses in "absolute" terms—always leave some doubt by showing that others may perceive it differently (even as an asset or strength).
- Qualify the weakness in the context of your overall performance (i.e., state that although an area for improvement, the weakness has not had significant impact on your overall job performance).

These are some of the main strategies you can employ to help you field "weaknesses" questions, and survive the potential damage that might otherwise be caused during the interview if improperly handled. Since Chapter 4 deals with this matter in great detail, there is no point in further expanding on this topic. If you have not already done so, I suggest that you carefully review Chapter 4 to learn how you can become even more skilled in successfully handling this potentially damaging and critically important area of the employment interview.

CLASSIC ANSWERS

You will see how the above techniques have been employed to minimize damage in the following classic answers to the "major weaknesses" category:

My two greatest job-related weaknesses are that I tend to be highly focused and results-oriented. Sometimes in my zeal to get things done I am not always as sensitive as I might be to the fact that others don't always have the same sense of urgency as I have. Some, therefore, may see me as "pushy." Others, however, would tell you that they like my positive attitude and enthusiasm.

* * *

The area I would most like to improve is my written communications skills. Although this has certainly not been an area of major concern, it is an area in which I would like to improve. I did take a creative writing workshop back in January, however, and know that I have experienced some improvement in this area. I am also looking into some writing courses at the Community College and plan to enroll this fall, workload permitting.

* * *

Although I know my boss is quite satisfied with my overall performance, one area suggested for improvement during my last performance review is my tendency to sometimes be too brief in report writing. This has certainly not been an area of major concern, since I know my boss has every confidence in my technical competence and the quality of my work. What I'm learning, however, is that my boss needs better documentation of what I am doing in the project for his own protection in the event something were to happen to me.

I can't blame him for that, so I am making a real effort to give him what he needs.

You can see by both the choice of topics and the way they are handled in the interview, these examples demonstrate how effectively the "weaknesses" question can be managed by a well-prepared employment candidate. In fact, with some careful planning, these difficult questions can be handled with relative ease and can often be turned into positive impressions, especially if you have already taken steps to improve yourself in the areas you cite for improvement.

7

INTERVIEW
QUESTIONS—
EDUCATION

KEY INTERVIEW QUESTIONS

E ducation has long been a common target of the interview and selection process, as employers examine the
qualifications of candidates for openings within their companies. There is a tendency for this to be a far more important component of the interview discussion for those who
are early in their career than for those who are well along
in their careers. In these cases, experience will represent
the lion's share of the focus, with education taking a back
seat.

Nonetheless, there will usually be a few questions concerning your educational qualifications incorporated into
most employer's interview designs. Here are some of the
questions that you might be asked:

- *Tell me about your education.*
- *What do you most value about your education? Why?*
- *How did your education prepare you for your career?*
- *How has your education been beneficial to your current job?*
- *In what way has your educational experience helped your job productivity?*
- *How relevant has your education been in preparing you for your profession?*
- *What could you do from an educational standpoint to improve your overall effectiveness in your work?*
- *What specific courses have proven most helpful to you in performing your job? How have they helped you?*
- *How did you select Bucknell University? What factors most influenced your decision?*
- *What led to your decision to choose your major?*
- *In which courses did you do best? Why?*
- *What were your worst courses? Why?*
- *What were the key benefits of attending Bucknell University?*
- *In what ways have you benefited from your decision to be an accounting major?*
- *What did you like most about your educational experience?*
- *What did you least like about your educational experience?*
- *If you could repeat your educational experience, what would you do differently? Why?*
- *What professor most influenced your life? Why?*
- *What was there about being an engineering major that you found most appealing?*
- *How have you used your education to your benefit?*
- *What aspects of your life has your education most influenced?*

- *How good a student were you? What accounted for this?*

As you can see from the variety of these interview questions, employers use the topic of education to gain insight about different aspects of your qualifications. Some examples are:

1. Questions concerning why you chose a particular school or major provide insight about how you think and make decisions (i.e., your decision-making process). Are you logical, thorough, and rational in how you make decisions, or are you impulsive and rely on intuition and convenience?

2. Questions about the key factors you used to select a given school or major provide some strong clues to employers about your basic value system. Did you select the school because of its excellent reputation in your field of study, or did you select it because of its reputation for providing a great social life? Did you select your major because of its relationship with something you really wanted to do with your life, or did you select it because it had a reputation as being a "complete breeze"? Each answer provides the employer with a different impression about what is important to you.

3. Questions about how you benefited from your education are sometimes used by employers as a way to gauge the level of your interest in your chosen occupation. If you show enthusiasm about how your education has helped you perform your job or helped to advance your career, it may demonstrate your enthusiasm and interest in your work. Persons who enjoy their work are usually far more productive than those who do not.

4. Interview questions about the benefits of your education are also sometimes used by the employer as a way of measuring your capacity to make practical application of your formal education and training. Practical application of knowledge to the solution of problems is

much of what the working world is about. Persons who can't seem to make this connection may be seen by some employers as "too theoretical" or "lacking practicality." Or, worse yet, some employers may view such candidates as simply not having sufficient "candlepower" to make the connection in the first place!

5. Interview questions about "best courses" and "worst courses" may also yield important information to the employer. On one hand, questions about your "best courses" (i.e., those that you most liked or those in which you got the best grades) may tell the employer something about your technical competency and your level of interest in the type of work they have to offer.

Courses that were well-liked, if related to the position for which you are interviewing, will suggest to the employer that you will probably be well motivated to do the work. Thus, if you particularly enjoyed your courses in thermodynamics and heat transfer, and you are applying for a job in engineering design with a manufacturer of industrial ovens, you are probably in pretty good shape. This suggests that you will be stimulated and motivated to perform the work they have to offer. Having good grades in thermodynamics and heat transfer will also suggest that you have the knowledge and technical competency to successfully perform the work as well. On the other hand, if you absolutely hated thermodynamics and heat transfer and these were your worst courses academically, you can bet there is going to be a far different interview outcome. In fact, you may well find the interview discussion politely cut short.

As you review the various questions that employers will use to probe the connection between your education and the work they have to offer, coupled with the above discussion, it should be evident that you will need to be well prepared to answer such inquiries if you are seriously interested in being on the receiving end of an employment offer. Failure to adequately address these questions is bound to have dire consequences for those candidates who are unprepared.

INTERVIEW STRATEGY

Good preparation for this interview component suggests that you will want to start by reviewing the sample questions provided here, making sure that you have prepared answers that will reflect well on your employment candidacy. Perhaps the best way to accomplish this (i.e., develop effective answers) is to focus on the key categories that comprise this area.

Let's systematically explore what are likely to be effective interview strategies for these each of these key areas.

Selection of School or Major

What you don't want to be doing here is to tell the employer things like, "I chose Penn State University because it was close to home." Or, "I chose Sociology because my friends told me that it was easy." Even though both answers may be truthful, this is not what you want to tell the employer if your heart is set on getting a job offer.

Think, instead, of other more constructive ways to answer these questions that will reflect more favorably on both your decision-making ability as well as the career-related interest in your major. I am not suggesting that you lie; however, I am suggesting that you come up with some alternate answers that will be more appealing to the employer. If you are going to win in this intensely competitive labor market, you are going to need to be rather commercial in the answers you supply.

Here are some ideas of alternate ways to answer this question:

Reasons for Choosing School

1. Excellent reputation as an institution where you could get a solid education.
2. Excellent reputation as being particularly strong in your major.
3. Good reputation for being a solid liberal arts school in addition to having strong courses in your specialty.

4. Wanted a larger school that would expose you to a wider range of backgrounds and viewpoints.

5. Wanted a larger school that had better resources and provided for more choices should you choose more narrow specialization later on.

6. Wanted a smaller school that would provide the opportunity for closer relationships with the faculty and more individualized attention (you would not be just a number).

7. You looked at several schools, and this one best suited your overall selection criteria:

   —has a solid reputation in your major.

   —provided a good mix of social backgrounds and viewpoints.

   —was priced at a level you could afford.

   —was within a day's driving time of home (a travel cost savings).

8. Describe the selection process (showing you were thorough, careful); for example:

   —Ordered literature from two dozen schools.

   —Read information on majors and school's overall focus.

   —Read information about school's overall environment.

   —Prepared list of key selection criteria (academic and nonacademic).

   —Narrowed list down to seven schools.

   —Visited all seven schools—took general tour, stayed overnight, attended classes in major, talked with several students, got names and contact information on recent graduates.

   —Called recent graduates regarding their impressions.

   —Selected school best matching your overall criteria.

Reasons for Choosing Major

1. You felt it was a logical choice for your combination of interests and skills.

2. Enjoyed the high school courses you had in this area, so felt you would enjoy this major.

3. Area was one that you always found interesting, and employment prospects appeared reasonable for this major.

4. Your research indicated that this was the preferred major for persons having your professional employment interests.

5. This area seemed very exciting, based upon related high school courses you'd had, and discussions with persons employed in that field.

How Education Has Helped or Benefited You

A good strategy here is to think about how your education has changed your overall or specific perspective about life and/or work. Speak about the "broadening" aspects of your education—how it has opened up your eyes to a broader ranges of possibilities and alternatives. Speak about how it has provided you with an understanding of how to research and get answers to problems in areas with which you are unfamiliar. Talk also about how it has opened up your thinking and receptivity to the ideas and approaches of others.

In the area of technical competency, talk about the specialized or technical knowledge you acquired through education that has enabled you to solve key problems with which you are now faced in the performance of your job. Cite specific examples of major problems you have successfully solved (or are prepared to solve) and the results you have achieved (or can likely achieve) in areas relevant to the position for which you are interviewing.

"Best" Versus "Worst" Courses

Once again, my advice is to be intelligent and commercial in answering questions concerning your "best" or "worst" courses. You will want to select those "best" courses that are most related to the job for which you are being interviewed.

One important distinction to remember when formulating your interview strategy is the difference between those courses you "liked" and those in which you "did well." Although the two normally go hand-in-hand, this may not always be the case. You can sometimes like a course, but not do particularly well in it. Conversely, you can sometimes do well in a course which you did not find particularly stimulating, Further, lack of interest or even how well you performed, may have had little to do with course content, and a lot to do with the professor or the way the course was taught.

You can elect to play these variables to your advantage (hence "be commercial") by the way you go about answering the question. If, for example you did poorly in thermodynamics and you are asked what your "best" course was, you could answer that you "particularly enjoyed" thermodynamics, and state the reasons why from a course content standpoint. On the other hand, if you didn't enjoy thermodynamics but did well in it, you could honestly state that your "best" course was thermodynamics, stating that you did particularly well in it citing the high grade that you received. In this case, there is no commercial value to sharing with the employer that you didn't like the course that much.

In the same vein, when asked about your "worst" courses, you are not going to want to select those which most directly related to the job for which you are interviewing. Try, in these cases, to select those that are the most unrelated and in which you had less interest. Try to avoid choosing courses in which your academic performance was sub par. This is not something you are going to want to focus the employer's attention on.

So, for example, if you are a science major, when asked to cite your "worst course," choose a course you took in the humanities field which was not particularly interesting but in which you did okay from a grade standpoint. By contrast, if you are a humanities major, you may want to cite a science course that you found uninteresting (but in which you got a "C" or better), in response to questions about your "worst" course. When asked "why" you did not like a particular course, it is best to cite course content or presentation as the principle. Avoid citing poor academic performance as the primary reason, since doing so, will only cause "red flags" (signs of danger) to go up for the employer.

Academic Performance

When asked about your overall academic performance, you are going to have little difficulty if you were a good student. This is particularly true if you did unusually well in those courses most related to the employer's areas of interest. You are going to want not only to cite your overall academic excellence, but also to highlight your performance in the relevant courses as well.

The greater difficulty comes if you were not a particularly good student, or if you did not do well grade-wise in those courses most relevant to the employer's requirements. Such poor academic performance may suggest a number of possibilities to the employer such as:

- You lack the technical competence necessary for successful job performance.
- You lack the basic intelligence to comprehend the material.
- You are poorly motivated.
- You lack good study habits.
- You lack sufficient discipline.
- You lack drive and perseverance.

When the issue is that you were simply not a strong student overall, the opportunity may still be readily salvageable depending on a number of possible counterbalancing circumstances. For example, if you did poorly during your first year or two but improved substantially the last two years, you might be able to chalk it up to immaturity and/or learning how to study better. In this case, you will want to highlight the degree of academic improvement during the last two years of your education. Also, if although you did not do well in general, but did particularly well in those courses most relevant to the employer's requirements, you can highlight those courses in which you did well and cite this trend as testimony to your solid training and interest in those areas most germane to the employer's needs. If handled well, both these strategies can serve as a strong counterbalance to your somewhat spotty academic record.

When factual, another possible hedge to poor academic performance could be the fact that your financial status required that you work a fairly healthy schedule in order to pay for your education. This is far more convincing when you can indicate that you paid for more than half your education through part-time employment while simultaneously attending classes.

When all else fails and you can offer no palatable explanation for your poor academic achievement, you might try some humor by citing the famous Princeton University study. This project supposedly studied over 10,000 graduates showing that there was no meaningful correlation between grade point average and career success. In this case, you can only hope that the interviewer appreciates your humor and is convinced that you are one of those individuals who could be cited as further evidence of the Princeton study's validity. Or, if you are lucky, perhaps the interviewer was also something less than a stellar student, and can both identify and sympathize with your plight.

CLASSIC ANSWERS

The following answers to education-related questions should prove beneficial as models for developing your own well-conceived answers to these same types of interview questions:

My decision for selecting Washington University was primarily based upon the excellent reputation of its School of Forestry among the leading companies in the forest products industry. Some basic research that I conducted through the American Forest Products Institute shows that the school is ranked only second to the Institute of Paper Chemistry as the leading pulp and paper school in the United States. Although the Institute of Paper Chemistry is certainly an excellent school, its emphasis is highly technical, and I wanted a less technical education that would serve to broaden my thinking. I felt that Washington fit the bill rather nicely.

* * *

I chose Ohio State because I felt a bigger university would offer a much larger selection of courses within my major and would also have the latest computer-related technology at its disposal. I've not been disappointed at all with my choice. The course selection has been extensive and the University is very up-to-date in terms of its computer-related resources. For me it was an excellent choice.

* * *

The choice of engineering was an easy one for me. In high school, I was an excellent student in math and science. I particularly enjoyed physics, which involved the application of math to scientific problems. Engineering, especially mechanical engineering, seemed a logical extension of my interest in physics.

* * *

In the broad sense, my education has helped me to learn how to be independent and solve problems with little or no assistance. It has taught me to how to think, how to analyze, and where to go to get the answers. More specifically, it provided me with solid grounding in accounting methods and principles, which has enabled me to perform at a high level as an accounting professional. It has given me a high level of confidence in my technical knowledge and ability.

* * *

My best course was the undergraduate course that I took in the Philosophy of Religions. As a theology major, it provided me with enormous insight into the reasoning behind the beliefs of the world's major religions. It also stretched my mind to consider the enormous number of possibilities that all seem to support the existence of a Supreme Being.

My worst course was Power and Politics. Although I did well in the course, I'm not sure that I see its relevance for someone like me who has chosen the ministry as my life's work.

*   *   *   **

Although my general academic performance has been average, I have done particularly well in business courses which, as you know, was my major. In fact, my grade point average in business courses is approximately 3.4. In marketing, I have done even better, with close to a 4.0. Marketing is clearly my strength and also my strongest interest.

8

INTERVIEW QUESTIONS— JOB PERFORMANCE

KEY INTERVIEW QUESTIONS

Sooner or later, the interviewer is bound to get around to asking you something about your job performance. This can be done in a number of ways, a few examples of which follow:

- *In checking with your boss, what would he tell me about your performance? What things would he say you do well? What improvements would he say could be realized?*
- *How well does your recent salary increase reflect your actual performance? Why?*
- *What changes have you brought to the job since entering the position?*
- *What would you list as being your three most significant accomplishments? In your current position? Since joining the company? In your career to-date?*

- *In talking with your co-workers, what would they cite as: Your biggest contributions to the department? The two areas where you could most improve your performance?*

- *What have your last three performance ratings been? Why?*

- *In what areas does your job performance excel?*

- *In what areas could your performance improve?*

- *Of which job accomplishments are you most proud? Why?*

- *Of what aspects of your performance are you least proud? Why?*

- *What were your key job objectives this past year, and how did you do against them?*

- *What evidence can you cite that demonstrates your job effectiveness?*

- *With what aspects of your performance are you least satisfied? What improvements could be realized? What steps have you taken to improve in these areas?*

- *What major accomplishments best demonstrate your qualifications for this position? Of which of these accomplishments are you most proud? Why?*

- *If your co-workers were asked to rate your overall performance on a scale of 1 to 10 (1 low, 5 average, 10 outstanding), what rating do you feel they would assign? Why? What factors would rate high? Why? What factors would rate low? Why?*

- *What aspects of your job performance would your boss rate as exceeding expectations? Why? Meeting expectations? Falling short of expectations? Why?*

- *Which of your accomplishments best exemplifies your qualifications for this position?*

- *How well does your job performance compare with others in your department? Where do you excel? Where could you improve?*

- *As you review your overall performance during the past year:*
  - *—Of which accomplishments are you most proud?*
  - *—Of what results are you least proud? Why?*
  - *—How would you categorize the quantity of your work? Why?*
  - *—How would you categorize your work quality? Why?*

Your job performance, as perceived by you, your boss, and your co-workers is bound to be an important area of focus during the course of the job interview. Interview theory subscribes to the basic principle that the best single predictor of future performance is one's past performance in the same or similar work. So the employer will closely probe all of the various dimensions of your past performance, as seen by the example questions, for clues as to how well you will perform the job for which you are being interviewed.

The questions shown here are very typical of those you can expect to encounter in most employment interviews. They are well-balanced, focusing on your performance achievements as well as performance shortfalls, as seen by both yourself as well as by others who are familiar with the quantity and quality of your work.

By asking these questions, for the most part, employers are looking for evidence in your current or past performance that you have the ability to meet the responsibilities of the job for which you are being considered. However, they are also looking for a history of solid performance and contribution suggesting that you are productive and motivated to bring constant improvement and value to the function.

A strong history of achievement and productivity has taken on increased significance in recent years, since in many recently downsized, reengineered organizations, managers are under the gun to produce more with fewer people and resources. They need to know, therefore, that they are hiring someone who will hit the ground running, and can work productively and efficiently.

INTERVIEW STRATEGY

When answering these questions, you need to paint a picture of someone who has historically been a strong performer and major contributor to the goals and objectives of the organization throughout his or her career. In preparing for this phase of the interview, therefore, it is important that you take some time in advance of the interview discussion to revisit your past positions and to delineate the key contributions that you have made.

Think about the formal goals and objectives that you and your boss had set, and how you performed against them. Which were met or exceeded, and what can be said, using quantitative terms, to demonstrate the degree of improvement brought about through your efforts? Also think in terms of key improvements that you initiated of your own volition, that were not part of any formal performance goal-setting process. In doing so, remember to ask yourself what problems existed at the time you first entered the position, and what you did to bring improvement in these areas.

When answering interview questions concerning areas where performance improvement could be realized, try to pick improvement areas that are least damaging and, for the most part, are unrelated to the position for which you are interviewing. Avoid highlighting performance shortfalls that suggest that you're not qualified or motivated to perform important aspects known to be crucial to performance success in the new job. Also, aim to select shortfalls that are fairly minor when compared to some of your more significant performance successes. Reinforce this idea by actually stating to the employer that these shortcomings were truly not viewed as major issues, due to the strength of your overall job performance.

CLASSIC ANSWERS

Here are some suggested answers that should prove helpful to you in structuring your own strategy for successfully addressing this area of the interview:

Kathy, I can honestly say that I have had a long history of above average performance. I think my history of frequent promotions offers good evidence that my current and past employers have been very satisfied with my work. I suppose, however, that my most significant failure occurred two years ago when, as project manager for the Virgo Project, we finished the project one month later than called for in the project plan.

This delay was caused by a steel strike with one of our major suppliers, who could not meet the delivery schedules on the structural steel needed for the plant's foundation. Since most suppliers were overcapacity and had significant order backlogs, we had a tough time finding a secondary supplier who was willing to interrupt production schedules to get us what we needed. However, after considerable effort, we were successful and managed to get a commitment.

Offsetting the delay, however, was the fact that we did bring the project in some 10 percent under budget. This saved the company nearly $2 million.

*   *   *

The accomplishment which in my judgment best demonstrates my qualifications for success as employment manager for your company is the 30 percent reduction in hiring costs realized by my company last year. This came about as a result of an incentive-based employee referral program which I initiated in an effort to reduce the fees that we had previously been paying to employment agencies. Total cost savings realized by my company are about $1.5 million annually.

*   *   *

The area most likely cited by co-workers for improvement of my performance would be impatience. I normally work at a fairly healthy clip, and may sometimes have a tendency to be impatient with others who like to work at a more leisurely pace. This tends to be especially true when we are working on a team project, and I must wait for key information that I need to carry out my portion of the effort. Although generally liked by my co-workers, I am sure that I am sometimes seen as being a little too impatient under these circumstances.

These examples will provide a good basis for developing an effective interview strategy for addressing interview questions designed to probe your overall job performance.

9

INTERVIEW QUESTIONS— WORK PREFERENCE

KEY INTERVIEW QUESTIONS

There are a myriad of ways the employer can explore your preference for certain types of work in an effort to determine your motivation to perform the job for which you are being interviewed. The following presents a good smattering of interview questions typically used by the interviewer to thoroughly explore this match:

- *From the standpoint of content, which of your past jobs have you enjoyed most? Why?*
- *As far as content is concerned, which of your past jobs did you least enjoy? Why?*
- *What type of work do you find rewarding and stimulating? Why?*
- *What type of work do you find least rewarding and stimulating? Why?*

- *Which of your past jobs provided the most interesting challenges? What were these challenges? What made them interesting?*

- *Which of your past jobs did you find least challenging? Why? What did you find unchallenging? What factors influenced your feelings?*

- *How would you describe the type of work you most like to do?*

- *How would you characterize the type of work that you least like doing?*

- *How would you compare the type of work you did at Berringer Corporation with the job content of your position at Weston Company? Which did you like better? Why? Which did you like least? Why?*

- *In which of your past positions were you most motivated and productive? What work factors accounted for your motivation? Which of these most affected your positive feelings? The absence of what factors also contributed to your positive outlook?*

- *Describe the type of work you would find most satisfying from a professional standpoint.*

- *Describe the type of work you would find least satisfying from a professional standpoint.*

- *What are some of the criteria you are using to determine whether or not a given job will be of interest to you?*

- *What has past work experience taught you about the type of work you most enjoy doing?*

- *What has such experience taught you about the kind of work you least like doing?*

- *What aspects of your current position do you find most enjoyable? Why?*

- *What aspects of your current position do you find least satisfying? Why?*

- *With what aspects of your past job at the XX Company were you most comfortable? With what aspects of this same position were you most uncomfortable?*

- *From the standpoint of job content, what factors most influence your level of job satisfaction? Which enhance satisfaction? Which diminish satisfaction?*
- *From the standpoint of job content, how would you describe your "ideal job"?*

The real intent behind these questions is to discover your motivation to perform the job. Employers have long known that having the technical qualifications and core competencies to perform the job is one thing; being motivated to do the work is something quite different. In the ideal world, employers have a preference for those candidates who are not only technically qualified to do the job but for whom the job will be rewarding and stimulating.

By asking you to compare and contrast different positions you have held in the past from a "likes versus dislikes" standpoint, the employer is looking for a consistent pattern for the type of work that you have historically found motivational. If the characteristics of this work coincide with the characteristics of the work for which you are being considered, the employer is inclined to feel that you will be equally motivated to perform the new job as well.

On the other hand, where the factors that caused you to dislike (or be less motivated by) past positions are present in the new position, the employer will feel that this will not be a good fit and an employment offer is not likely to be forthcoming. The deduction is that you will be equally unhappy with and not motivated to perform the new job as well.

INTERVIEW STRATEGY

You will want to be commercial in your answer to this one. Before going to the interview, give some quality thought to the type of work for which you will be interviewing from the standpoint of actual job content. Think your way through those aspects of the new job that you are likely to most enjoy, and be sure to highlight these factors when asked to describe those factors that are important to your job satisfaction.

Likewise, when asked to rank your past jobs from a job satisfaction standpoint, be sure to choose those jobs that are most similar in content to the position for which you are interviewing. Don't make the mistake of highlighting a similar job as being the one that you liked least. Doing so will quickly close the curtain as far as the prospects for landing this position are concerned.

Also be careful how you describe those past positions that you "least enjoyed." You don't want to appear to be a classic malcontent, someone who is never quite satisfied. Nothing will end an interview sooner. Make sure the employer understands that you didn't "dislike" the job; you simply "liked it less" than other positions you have held. When discussing this "least liked" job, present a balanced assessment, also talking about those aspects of the job that you found rewarding and stimulating. This will suggest to the employer that you are far more adaptive and flexible than if you only talked about the factors that you found unappealing.

CLASSIC ANSWERS

The following can serve as examples of ways this series of questions might be answered effectively:

> *Actually, Barbara, I have enjoyed certain aspects of all of the positions I have held. It is difficult to pick one that I enjoyed least. I suppose in drawing a fine line of distinction between the positions, I would have to choose the position at Hawthorne Company. Although I generally liked this job, it was fairly well-defined and there did not appear to be as much flexibility to bring about changes as some of the other positions I have held. I suppose this was a drawback, but certainly not a serious one.*

* * *

> *Jobs that I find most rewarding and stimulating are those where I have the opportunity to use a combination of analytical and creative skills. My psychological*

profile rates me particularly strong in both categories. I tend to thrive in those jobs offering the opportunity to tackle major, long-standing problems that the employer has a strong desire to solve. This tends to challenge and stimulate me.

(*Note:* This answer assumes that the job for which the candidate is interviewing provides these kinds of challenges.)

*   *   *

Of the positions I have held, the job that I most liked was Manager of Technical Employment for Jones Chemical Corporation. Jones was doubling its size in two years, requiring me to recruit better than 200 engineers to support the expansion.

I tend to like jobs that are demanding and require getting a lot of work done in a fairly short time frame. I like the problem-solving challenge of figuring out creative ways to get the job done, even when it would appear to be an all-but-impossible task. By the way, I was able to fill all 200 positions in the time required to meet the project deadlines.

Notice, in these answers, how the candidate tended to emphasize the positive and de-emphasized the negative when discussing "least liked" positions. Care was taken to avoid saying he or she disliked the job. Instead, the candidate presented a more balanced view, stating that there were certain aspects of the job that he or she liked as well.

You will also notice, when describing most-liked jobs, how the candidates in these examples took this opportunity to further market particular skills and assets that related to the aspects of the job that he or she most enjoyed.

10

INTERVIEW QUESTIONS— MOTIVATION AND DRIVE

KEY INTERVIEW QUESTIONS

Employees who possess drive and motivation have always been in high demand by employers. These two traits go hand-in-hand with efficiency and productivity which, from the employer's standpoint, are the primary objectives of an effective employee/employer relationship. As a consequence, you can almost bet on the fact that some of the interview questions you encounter during the course of your employment interview will be aimed at measuring the extent of your drive and motivation.

Here are some examples of such interview questions:

- *Give me some examples of your accomplishments that go well beyond the absolute requirements of your current job.*

- *What basis do you use for measuring your own performance?*
- *What are you currently doing to improve your overall job performance?*
- *How do you measure your personal success?*
- *What are some of your personal job-related goals?*
- *What are your three most important job objectives, and why are they important?*
- *How does your current performance measure up to your personal standards? What do you want to improve? What are you doing to improve in these areas?*
- *Tell me about your process for setting goals and objectives. What are the basic steps of this process? How do you choose your objectives?*
- *How has your performance measured up to expectations? Did you meet objectives? Exceed objectives? Greatly exceed objectives? Fall short of objectives?*
- *How would you describe your work ethic and performance compared with your functional peers?*
- *What are your long-term goals and objectives?*
- *What major changes and improvements do you want to bring about within your function in the next year or two?*
- *What can you tell me about yourself that best illustrates your personal drive and motivation?*
- *What do you believe are the three or four most important principles needed to achieve job success?*
- *What do you believe are the common characteristics of highly successful people?*

When employers attempt to measure a candidate's drive and motivation, they frequently look for those things the candidate has accomplished that go beyond the basic requirements of the position. Almost by definition, people who possess a high level of drive and motivation tend to go well beyond these fundamental requirements and are continuously striving to bring about improvement in both their overall job performance and in themselves personally. They have a strong dedication to achieving excellence and are willing to make the personal sacrifices that go along with such commitment.

A common characteristic of well-motivated people is that they are normally goal-oriented. They are driven to set both job and personal goals and have high expectations of their own performance. Such individuals are self-motivated and as such are prone to continuously measure their own performance, without prompting, against the goals they have set for themselves. In addition, their goals tend to be more ambitious than others who lack the same degree of motivation. They usually set more difficult goals and will also take on a larger overall workload than their less-motivated counterparts.

Another known characteristic common to persons who have high level of drive is that they tend to be ambitious about their own careers. They have a strong need to succeed personally and are dedicated to their personal development. It is not uncommon for such individuals to have assessed their own development needs and to have formulated a plan that will enable them to develop the skills and capabilities they will need for career success.

Finally, candidates who are well-motivated also exhibit a clear sense of urgency and a strong drive for rapid completion. There is a sense of energy and urgency about them that is evident almost immediately. They speak with great energy and enthusiasm about their work and exhibit a certain electricity and magnetism. They tend to excite and energize those around them with their positive attitude and enthusiasm.

Since employers are very much tuned-in to the characteristics and tendencies just discussed, they will look for evidence of these same attributes throughout the interview. This is particularly true in today's environment where, due to extensive downsizing and severely reduced staffs, most hiring managers have an intensified need to hire highly motivated, productive people. However, it has always been true that employers have a strong preference for those candidates who exhibit drive and motivation over their less-motivated peers.

INTERVIEW STRATEGY

Review of the interview questions presented earlier in this section suggests that to be effective at fielding interview questions having to do with your motivation and drive, you will need to be prepared to show evidence of these desired characteristics in the following ways:

1. Through the challenging business goals that you have set.
2. Through the ambitious personal goals that you have set.
3. By citing unique or outstanding accomplishments.
4. By citing results achieved that go well beyond basic job requirements.
5. By demonstrating your willingness to take on a large workload.

Nothing will bring havoc to interview success faster than, when asked about your business goals, you are unable to point to any. Such response will send a clear message to the employer about your motivation. However, it is not likely to be the message you would prefer to send.

So, if you don't already have business and personal goals, there is no time like the present to set them. You will want to be prepared to enthusiastically talk about these goals, and their potential impact on business and personal effectiveness.

Since employers, in looking for well-motivated people, are going to look for evidence of unusual accomplishment, you will want to scour your past accomplishments for those that stand out from the ordinary. Be prepared to talk convincingly about the difficulty of achieving these objectives and their significant impact on the organization for which you worked. The ability to achieve significant accomplishments against great odds speaks volumes about your drive and motivation—a message that will not fall on deaf ears.

CLASSIC ANSWERS

This area is a little more difficult to illustrate than some of the past topics. This is primarily due to the difficulty of conveying the level or degree of motivation in the context of the work being performed. Persons not working in a particular field may have difficulty understanding the significance of a particular accomplishment or goal since they have no frame of reference and, for this reason, may be unable to fully appreciate the level of energy and motivation needed to attain these results.

Hopefully, however, the following representative examples will give you some idea on how to approach the subject:

One accomplishment that exceeded my basic job requirements was the reduction of department operating costs by some 60 percent, far more than was expected of me. Each department manager was given a cost reduction goal of 25 percent to accomplish by year end. We went considerably beyond that target through some creative, major reengineering and work redesign along with automation of several of our work processes. Annual savings to the business was about $0.25 million.

* * *

Some of my personal job-related goals include reducing standing inventories by at least 90 percent and working toward a just-in-time delivery system with our raw materials suppliers. I estimate annual savings to the business to be in the range of $3 million. We are hard at work on this one and expect to have things pretty much in place within the next 3 months.

A second personal goal that I have is to work with Engineering to automate the product packaging area. We are still handpacking cases in this area to get a mixed color assortment per case. Preliminary investigation of automatic packaging equipment that I have undertaken suggests that we could reduce labor costs by nearly $0.75 million per year. We just received capital authorization for this project, but I expect to have this equipment in-place and fully operational within six weeks.

* * *

If you talked with my boss, she would confirm that I have exceeded all expectations during the last two years. We jointly set some very aggressive objectives for the year, all of which were met, with most accomplished reasonably ahead of schedule. Additionally, I undertook two other major projects beyond those to which we had agreed, and I believe both will have been completed before we reach year end.

* * *

One of my key personal objectives is to complete a part-time M.B.A. program over the next two years. I am already halfway through. I feel this will provide me with a much broader range of knowledge in other business areas such as marketing and finance. I have a strong desire to learn more about the overall operation of businesses and what is really important to creating a successful enterprise. As a part of my learning, I also try to read at least one business-related book a month. I always pick topics with which I am unfamiliar. This forces me to keep expanding my intellectual horizons, and serves to stretch my mind a bit.

11

INTERVIEW QUESTIONS— PERSONAL TRAITS AND CHARACTERISTICS

KEY INTERVIEW QUESTIONS

Self-descriptive questions are frequently asked by the employer to gain some insight into the candidate's personal style. The following are typical of questions you can expect to encounter in the interviewer as the employer attempts to gauge your personal style—your key traits and characteristics:

- *How would you describe yourself?*
- *What five or six adjectives best describe you?*
- *If we were to ask two or three of your co-workers to describe you, what would they likely say?*
- *If we asked your boss to list three or four of your most positive attributes, what would he or she tell us?*

- *What traits and characteristics would your boss describe as less pleasing?*
- *What words best describe your personal style?*
- *Which of your personal traits and characteristics have proven most beneficial to your career?*
- *Which personal traits and characteristics have most hindered your career progress?*
- *During past performance reviews, which of your personal traits and characteristics have most often been cited as strengths?*
- *During such reviews, which of your personal traits and characteristics have been cited as areas for improvement?*
- *In your most intimate conversations with family and close friends, what have people said they most like about you?*
- *In similar conversations, what aspects of your personal style have been suggested as areas for improvement?*
- *Which of your traits and characteristics do you personally find most frustrating?*
- *Of which of your traits and characteristics are you most proud? Why?*
- *Of which of your traits and characteristics are you least proud? Why?*
- *What is there about yourself that you would most like to change? What change would you make? Why?*
- *Which of your personal traits and characteristics most enhance your effectiveness with others?*
- *Which of your personal traits and characteristics sometimes gets in the way of your relationship with others?*
- *Which of your personal traits and characteristics best qualify you for this job?*
- *Of which aspects of your personal style are you most sensitive and are you most trying to improve?*

Personal traits and characteristics are yet another dimension of cultural fit from the employment interview perspective. Asking about traits and characteristics gives employers a sense of your preferred behaviors and personal style. Employers will attempt to determine how well such characteristics and behaviors will fit their work environment. By asking these kinds of questions, they are attempting to determine how effective you are likely to be in your working relationships within that environment.

As an example of this, a person who is characterized as being "analytical, thorough, and cautious" may not be seen as a particularly good bet for a business start-up environment, where characteristics such as being "decisive, fast-acting, entrepreneurial, and risk-taking" are seen as premium attributes for successful performance. On the other hand, someone whose key attributes are those of being "decisive, fast-acting, entrepreneurial, and risk-taking" may well be seen as undesirable by a mature organization where someone with a more "cautious, analytical" style is preferred. The same identical traits can be seen differently by different organizations.

This does not mean that certain personal traits or attributes are wrong or undesirable. It really all depends on the nature of the work and organizational culture. What are seen as positive characteristics in one organization may well be viewed as negative by another.

INTERVIEW STRATEGY

As already mentioned, the differences in cultures and value systems can well determine whether or not a certain personal style or profile will be acceptable. Good interview strategy suggests that you must first find out something about the culture of the organization in which you will be working, and what kinds of traits, characteristics, and behaviors it prefers and rewards.

As with my previous recommendations concerning fit with the work environment of a prospective employer, in order to forge a winning interview strategy here, you will need to take the "cultural temperature" of the organization before your arrival (if you are fortunate enough to know persons employed there), or at the inception of the interview discussion.

Without some advance insight concerning the organization's preferences for certain characteristics and behaviors, your chances of succeeding are no better than hitting the bullseye on a dart board at a hundred paces while blindfolded.

Some preliminary questions you may want to seek answers to are as follows. These will serve to shed some insight concerning the employer's expectations:

- *What kinds of people are typically most successful in your work environment here at the Crosby Company?*

- *Considering the company's value system, what personal traits and characteristics seem to be important to doing well and fitting in?*

- *When you think about high performers here at Crosby, what are some of the unique traits and characteristics that set them apart from others?*

- *Each organization has its own unique culture. How would you describe the culture here at Baxter? What is important to fitting in and doing well in this culture?*

It should be fairly obvious that answers to these and similar questions can go a long way toward helping you to formulate a winning interview strategy. By knowing the preferred personal profile in advance, you have an opportunity to slant your self-description to fit the desired attributes of these those who are successful in the organization. The similarity of such descriptions will not escape the employer, who would certainly like to add another "Kentucky Derby winner" to the stable.

If you are unable to get this kind of advance intelligence or if the interviewer skillfully avoids answering your exploratory questions at the beginning of the interview, you will have to take your chances. You are probably reasonably safe to select those universal virtues and attributes that most organizations would be hard-pressed to criticize. These include such traits and characteristics as being open, honest, flexible, adaptable, friendly, hard-working, dedicated, loyal, results-oriented, and so on. It is pretty difficult to argue with these.

CLASSIC ANSWERS

Although different organizations will require different answers, the following sample answers are illustrative of some approaches you could take to answering these kinds of questions:

The three adjectives that, in my opinion, best describe me are creative, energetic, and result-oriented. I have earned a good reputation for coming up with creative solutions and ideas to solve difficult problems. I tend to get a lot accomplished in a relatively short time.

* * *

I think my co-workers would likely describe me as neat, well-organized and highly dependable. I seem to have a real propensity for making order out of disorder, and bringing a sense of efficiency and focus to the work environment. I've forgotten who said it, but I guess I am a strong believer in the saying, "A cluttered desk reflects a cluttered mind." Although I can function well in the midst of chaos, sooner or later, I will get it organized and gain a sense of control and efficiency.

* * *

Perhaps the single trait that has gotten in my way in the past has been a tendency to sometimes be a little too impatient and aggressive. I tend to be very hard-working and result-oriented, and sometimes in my desire to get things done quickly and efficiently, some may have viewed me as being somewhat pushy or aggressive. Although certainly never a major issue, I have attempted to be more sensitive to this tendency and have been working on it. I think I have managed to temper things quite a bit, and am now much more tolerant and patient than I used to be. Today, I think I can honestly say that I am no longer seen as being this way by others.

* * *

I think my boss would describe me as positive, energetic, and having a strong influence on the group. No matter how dire the circumstances, I always manage to maintain focus on the "positive possibilities." I just refuse to let things get me down. I enjoy the challenge of turning negatives into positives. As a result, I believe I serve as an inspiration to others, and they like having me around. I also tend to put a lot of positive energy into turning the corner and bringing positive results about. To me, that's the real challenge and the reason why we're here.

These examples will also serve as an inspiration to you in building a convincing story to tell employers about your positive traits, characteristics, and attributes, and how they will be of benefit to the organization.

12

INTERVIEW QUESTIONS— INTERPERSONAL SKILLS

KEY INTERVIEW QUESTIONS

Interpersonal skills, or how well one relates to and works with others, have long been a major focus area for candidate interviewing and selection. Questions that you are likely to encounter during the interview as the basis for examining your interpersonal skills include:

- *With what kind of persons do you most enjoy working? Why?*
- *With what kind of people do you have most difficulty working? Why?*
- *Describe your relationship with your boss.*
  - *—In what areas do you agree?*
  - *—In what areas do you disagree? Why?*
  - *—How do you resolve your differences?*

- *With which of your past co-workers did you most enjoy working? Why?*
- *What factors most influence these positive feelings?*
- *With which of your past co-workers did you least enjoy working?*

  —What accounted for your dissatisfaction?

  —What did you do about it?

  —What was the outcome of your efforts?
- *How would you describe your relationships with others outside your immediate work group?*
- *Tell me about a time when you had a major conflict with another employee.*

  —What caused the conflict?

  —What did you do to resolve the issue?

  —What were the results?
- *In which of your past positions did you feel most comfortable (had a sense of belonging and fitting in)? Why?*
- *In which of your past positions did you feel least comfortable (had a sense of not belonging and fitting in)? What most contributed to your uneasiness? What did you do to ease these feelings?*
- *During a reference check, what is your boss most likely to tell me about your interpersonal skills?*
- *In what areas would you be described as effective? What areas would be cited for improvement? Why?*
- *How could you most improve your interpersonal effectiveness?*
- *When confronted with an angry person, what do you do?*
- *If someone is critical of you and appears not to like you, what do you do?*
- *If you sensed you were not fitting in well with your work group and felt you were being treated as an outsider, what would you do?*

- *What examples can you cite that best demonstrate your ability to relate well to others?*
- *In which of your past positions did you feel most isolated and alone?*
  —What caused these feelings?
  —What did you do?
- *What could you do that would most improve your ability to relate to others?*
- *Which of your skills would you rate higher? Why?*
  —Your "technical" skills?
  —Your interpersonal skills?
- *Do you feel it is more important to be well-liked by others or be admired for your effectiveness? Why?*

Review of these interview questions shows a systematic approach that is frequently used to measure four dimensions of your interpersonal skills or ability to relate effectively to others. These are:

1. General ability to relate to others.
2. Ability to fit in with your work group.
3. Flexibility and adaptability.
4. Resourcefulness in dealing with conflict.

Employers generally seek individuals who are socially well-adjusted and have had a good history of working effectively with others. They also look for persons who are flexible and adaptable in their styles, and can make the necessary adjustments to fit in with just about any group they will need to work with. Persons who have demonstrated a trend of not fitting in and exhibit an inability to adapt to a wide range of styles and personalities are quickly screened out by skilled interviewers. Such individuals are seen as a high risk by most employers and will be carefully avoided.

The ability to successfully resolve conflict is often the theme of many interview questions in the interpersonal questions set. Employers have a clear preference for those with flexible styles and who have the resourcefulness to try several different approaches to resolving differences with others. Organizational conflict is inevitable, and the ability to successfully resolve conflict and build healthy, effective relationships is something that is valued and sought after by employers.

INTERVIEW STRATEGY

You will want to avoid any indication that you have had a history of difficulty dealing with others. In general, you will want to leave the employer with the impression that you are someone who gets along exceptionally well with others— that you are flexible, adaptive, and that you have the ability to build bridges and successfully resolve conflict with others. In a few words, you will want to demonstrate that you are a person who builds effective, harmonious working relationships with others, and that you are confident, positive, and socially well-adjusted.

When asked to cite areas for improvement in your interpersonal skills, you will want to start by first stating that you have a reputation for getting along well with others, and that interpersonal skills is one of your strengths. Then follow this with an improvement area that would be seen as fairly benign. In introducing this improvement need, paraphrase the introduction by using words such as "sometimes I have a tendency to . . ." This is far less absolute and suggests to the employer that this is only an occasional problem, and therefore not likely a major issue.

If asked to cite a circumstance when you had a major conflict with someone, pick a situation where you were successful in resolving the conflict. This will serve as a positive demonstration of your interpersonal skills and ability to build harmonious and effective working relationships. Citing an example of an unresolved conflict may suggest to the employer that you don't get along well with others, and that you lack the necessary desire, flexibility, and skills to build healthy, effective working relationships with others.

CLASSIC ANSWERS

The following represent some fairly effective ways of answering some of the tougher interview questions concerning your interpersonal effectiveness. They should serve as good models for preparing your own interview strategy for effectively addressing this interview set:

Mary, I have always had an excellent reputation for getting along well with others and view this as one of my strengths. Although this has certainly never been an issue, occasionally I could listen more carefully to another's point. Sometimes I may have a tendency to cut conversation short due to the crush of the workload. Realizing this, I have tried to consciously be sensitive to this tendency and force myself to be a little more patient. As result, I believe that I have improved in this area.

* * *

Yes, I've had one or two occasions where I have had a major blow-out with another employee, but fortunately I have always been able to successfully resolve them. These are very rare occasions, however.

Last year, while Manager of Technical Employment, I was accused by the director of human resources—technology of not producing sufficient employment candidates for the R&D group. He had just come back from a staff meeting with the vice president of technology in which this was raised as a major issue. Unfortunately, he assumed that I was to blame and came storming into my office full of anger and accusations.

I listened carefully and then, at the appropriate moment, cut in and said, "Jim, I can appreciate that you are upset. Perhaps if you can give me a minute or two we can get this thing ironed out." At this point, he calmed down and I was able to demonstrate that our log showed that we had sent over 300 resumes to various R&D managers for review that had not been returned. I was also able to show him several follow-up notes to these managers asking that the resumes be reviewed and returned.

Since at the time our department was the staffing resource to Central Engineering for a $1.5 billion capital program and had more than 150 engineering positions to fill, we were extremely busy. After realizing what we were up against and providing Jim with the evidence of our efforts to satisfy R&D's needs, Jim was quite satisfied and apologized for his behavior. I then gave him copies of the resume referral log for use in the vice president's next staff meeting. Needless to say, the problem disappeared shortly thereafter.

*   *   *

Although I have generally gotten along well with all of the groups I have worked in, the group with which I least enjoyed working with was the Cost Accounting Department at the Waynesboro mill. Although I certainly fit in with the group just fine and there were no real issues, I felt that they were not particularly motivated to bring about improvements in manufacturing cost reduction. They seemed more interested in being whistle blowers than a helpful resource to the operating department heads. This always made me feel a bit uncomfortable because of the animosity caused by this approach.

Quite frankly, I pretty much ignored this and went about my work. It was my approach, however, to work as a team with operating department managers, and to try to help them better understand and control their operating costs. I know they appreciated this and valued me as a professional resource to their team.

These examples will give you some good ideas for fashioning your own interview strategy in effectively addressing questions relating to your interpersonal skills. This is an important area for which you will need to be well-prepared if you are going to be successful in generating interest in your employment candidacy and landing job offers.

13

INTERVIEW QUESTIONS— PREFERRED WORK ENVIRONMENT

KEY INTERVIEW QUESTIONS

Compatibility with work environment is often a major focal area for employers during the interview and selection process. Employers want to determine if the candidate will be comfortable with the overall environment of the organization in which they will be working. Here are some questions used by employers in the interview to measure such "organizational fit":

- *In which past work environment were you happiest?*
  —Why were you happy?
  —What factors most influenced your feelings?
- *In which past work environment were you least happy?*
  —Why were you unhappy?
  —What factors most influenced your feelings?

- *How would you compare the work environment at Wilson Company with the work environment at Chilton?*

  —Which was more satisfying? Why?

  —Which was least satisfying? Why?

- *What did you like most about the work environment at Bower Corporation?*

- *What did you like least about the work environment at Bower Corporation?*

- *What aspects about the work environment at Johnson & Johnson did you find most stimulating? Why?*

- *What aspects about the work environment at Johnson & Johnson did you find least stimulating? Why?*

- *In which past work environment did you feel you had the most influence and impact?*

- *In which past work environment did you feel you had the least influence and impact? What caused these feelings?*

- *What type of work environment do you find motivational and stimulating? Why?*

- *What type of work environment do you find unstimulating and demotivating? Why?*

- *How could your current work environment be made more interesting and exciting?*

  —What things need to be changed?

  —In what way would you change them?

- *On a scale of 1 to 10 (1 low, 5 average, 10 high), where do you rate your level of satisfaction with your current work environment?*

  —What factors do you rate high? Why?

  —What factors do you rate low? Why?

- *In what kind of work environment are you most productive? Why?*

- *In what kind of work environment are you least productive? Why?*

- *What 4 or 5 things are most important to you in a work environment?*

    —Which is the most important? Why?

    —Which is the least important? Why?

- *How would you describe the "ideal" work environment?*

    —What would be present? Why?

    —What would be absent? Why?

- *Which of your past work environments has come closest to your "ideal"?*

    —What factors were most appealing?

    —How would you rank their importance? Why?

- *Describe the work environment in which you were most productive.*

    —What contributed to your effectiveness?

    —Which factors were most influential?

- *How would you describe your current work environment?*

    —What do you find satisfying? Why?

    —What improvements would you like to see? Why?

How well one aligns with the work environment or culture of the organization can often have significant impact on his or her effectiveness in the job. In many ways, organizations are truly sociopolitical systems. Although many organizations tout their commitment to supporting diversity, the reality is that almost all have a central philosophy, a core value system, and a preference for certain styles of behavior that are deemed desirable. The reward systems of most organizations, in fact, are designed to support these key values and behavioral styles.

Selecting individuals who do not share the common values and preferred behaviors supported by the organization leads to performance problems faster than you can say jack rabbit. Such individuals are thought to have "radical ideas," "don't fit in well," "are argumentive," "noncooperative," "not team-oriented," "opinionated," "stubborn," "not supportive" of organizational goals," and a whole host of other less-than-complimentary adjectives. Although such individuals may be very competent technically, their lack of congruency with the basic values and principles of the organization renders them ineffective. They have great difficulty getting management support for their ideas and in acquiring the resources needed to support their efforts.

Employers have long realized the importance of organizational fit. Through the use of questions such as those shown, they will normally attempt to select those individuals who will be most comfortable in the current work environment. To do this, they must first determine the type of work environment in which the candidate has historically been most productive and satisfied. They then compare that work environment to their own work environment to determine whether or not there is an appropriate match.

INTERVIEW STRATEGY

It is difficult to have a winning interview strategy here unless you have a clear understanding of the employer's culture almost from the beginning of the interview. How else could you possibly understand what the employer will be looking for and prepare an appropriate strategy?

This suggests that you need to get a reading on the work environment either before the interview actually begins or, in the event this is not possible, early in the interview discussion. Basic questions, such as the following, can help you to get a fix on this:

1. *What is it like to work in this environment?*
2. *What is particularly important to success?*
3. *What makes the culture of this organization different from others in which you have worked?*
4. *How would you describe the basic value system of this organization?*
5. *What kinds of values and behaviors are rewarded? What kinds of values and behaviors do not receive support?*

Where possible, such questions should be asked near the beginning of the interview discussion so that you have a clearer understanding of the traits, characteristics, values, and behaviors that will be seen as favorable in an employment candidate. It will also provide some good intelligence on what values and behavioral styles will be frowned upon by the organization. This allows you to adjust your strategy accordingly, providing the employer with the most appropriate answers to these questions.

If you want to win in the interview, you will want to choose to describe those past work environments as the ones "most liked" that best match the environment of the company with which you are interviewing. Choosing a different type culture as being the one you most prefer just doesn't make good commercial sense. It certainly is not going to get you the job offer.

On the other hand, "winning isn't everything." Forcing yourself into a culture in which you are going to be miserable is certainly not anyone's idea of winning. You may win the interview, but the price you pay in terms of unhappiness is bound to take a tremendous toll on you emotionally. In my opinion, life is too short to invite this kind of misery.

In answering the questions about "most satisfying" and "least satisfying" work environments, you will want to present a well-balanced view. Describing yourself as "extremely unhappy" in certain past work environments will surely raise some red flags on the part of the interviewer, suggesting that you do not posses the skills to readily adapt to a less-than-satisfying situation. It is best to temper your description of this dissatisfaction by being sure that the interviewer understands that there were aspects, even of this least-liked organization, that you found quite acceptable. This suggests that you are not a person who is "overly critical," and that you have some reasonable ability to adapt to your surroundings.

CLASSIC ANSWERS

The classic answers will depend upon the nature of the work environment of the organization with whom you are interviewing. A successful strategy will need to adapt to this organizational profile. However, be sure to present a balanced view, even if you absolutely hated one of the organizations in which you worked. Even in this case, look for the silver lining:

I can honestly say that I have enjoyed working for all of my past employers, so it is difficult to pick one over the other. I suppose if I had to split hairs, I would say that I found the environment at Hobart Corporation the least satisfying, although I was certainly not unhappy there. At Hobart, management tended to be a little more autocratic. Therefore, as employees, we tended to have a little less freedom to act than in some of the other companies for whom I have worked. This was not a major issue for me, however.

* * *

The factors that most influenced my positive feelings about working at Mifflin Corporation were its willingness to push decision making to the lowest level of the organization, and its commitment to employee development. The company seemed bent on making the fullest use of the capability of its people. As a result, both morale and productivity of the company were unusually high. Unfortunately, there was an unfriendly takeover by the Bowers Company, and most of our positions were eliminated.

* * *

I probably found working at Loudder Corporation the least satisfying. Although I certainly wasn't totally unhappy there, my boss was ready for retirement and "stacked arms" so to speak. It was difficult, as a result, to get him to support any new initiatives that would bring significant change. Although he was certainly a nice guy to have as a boss, I tend to be happier working for someone who is more interested in bringing about major changes and improvements in the way things are done. Ray just didn't have the heart for these kinds of changes at this stage of his career.

You can readily see from these examples how presenting a balanced view can reflect positively on your candidacy if effectively utilized. Try, therefore, never being overly critical of any past work environment in which you have worked. Presenting something positive about such environments speaks volumes about your positive attitude and flexibility—two factors that most employers highly value in an employment candidate.

14

INTERVIEW QUESTIONS— PREFERRED BOSS'S STYLE

KEY INTERVIEW QUESTIONS

It is certainly not at all uncommon during the typical employment interview to be asked about your relationship with your boss. Answers to these questions provide the employer with insight about your interpersonal effectiveness as well as the kind of boss for whom you prefer working.

The following are examples of questions you are likely to be asked on this subject during the course of your employment interview:

- *Who was the best boss you ever had? Why?*
- *What were some of this boss's key traits and characteristics?*
- *What effect did these have on you? Why?*

- *Describe your current boss. What do you most like about him or her? Why? What do you least like about him or her? Why?*
- *How would you describe your relationship with your current boss?*

  —In what areas do you most agree? Why?

  —In what areas do you disagree? Why?
- *If there was something you could change about your boss, what would it be? Why?*
- *What aspect of your boss's management style is most motivating? Why?*
- *What aspects of your boss's management style do you find demotivating? Why?*
- *How would you categorize your "ideal boss"?*

  —Describe his or her management philosophy.

  —Describe his or her management style.

  —Why do you prefer this style and philosophy?
- *How would you categorize the "worst boss" you could have?*

  —Describe his or her management philosophy.

  —Describe his or her management style.

  —In what ways would this profile be detrimental to you?

  —What would be demotivational about this style?
- *How would you characterize the traits and attributes of a good boss? Why are these important?*
- *How would you characterize the traits and attributes of a poor boss?*
- *What type of boss would you find motivating and stimulating? Why?*
- *What type of boss would you find demotivating and unstimulating? Why?*
- *Describe your relationship with your last boss.*
- *What did you most like about this boss? Why?*
- *What did you least like about this boss? Why?*

- *What is characteristic of the best bosses you have had? What do they have in common?*
- *What is characteristic of the worst bosses you have had? What do they have in common?*
- *Which of your past bosses would you most like to emulate? Why?*

When asking questions of this type, the employer usually has more than a single objective. The first is fairly straightforward, which is to ascertain the kind of boss for whom you enjoy working, The second is to determine something about your interpersonal effectiveness.

When asking about the traits and characteristics of your "most liked" or "best" boss, the employer is attempting to determine whether or not you will be compatible with your potential new boss. If you describe your best boss as someone who worked closely with you to clearly define objectives and to define the specifics of how things were to be done, this may suggest that you would not be a good match for a boss whose style it is to simply provide broad direction and let the subordinate determine the details of how things are to be done. Conversely, if your preference is to work for someone with a strongly participative style, and the new boss is one who prefers to manage through tight supervision and control, this also has a high probability for conflict and failure.

Performance success often hinges upon having a good relationship with the boss. If the two of you share similar workstyles and beliefs, you are far more likely to get the boss's support for your ideas as well as the resources you will need to carry out these ideas. Both are absolutely critical to performance success. Employers would prefer not to leave this relationship to chance, and will thus use the interview to eliminate those whose profiles appear incompatible.

Additionally, it is known that the compatibility of styles between boss and subordinate has significant impact on employee motivation and morale. Where these styles are compatible, the new employee will tend to be highly motivated and productive. On the other hand, when the two are at odds, the employee is likely to be demotivated and relatively nonproductive. From the employer's viewpoint, why take the risk when there are plenty of other well-qualified candidates available whose profiles are a good match with the boss's management style and philosophy? Most employers are unwilling to take such a risk.

A particularly poor relationship between an employment candidate and a current or past boss may also raise some additional "red flags" on the part of the prospective employer. Answers to follow-up questions about the causes of this less-than-perfect relationship may suggest to the employer that the candidate has difficulty getting along with others. Under these circumstances, the candidate's interpersonal skills are likely to come under suspicion, and there are a whole host of additional questions that will probably come into play, such as:

- *What was the cause of the poor relationship?*
- *Who was to blame?*
- *Is the candidate inflexible, that is, rigid in his or her style and unable to successfully adapt to persons with a different style or viewpoint?*
- *How resourceful was the candidate in attempting to accommodate and resolve the differences?*
- *Was the candidate either too passive or too aggressive in his or her attempt to confront the boss and resolve their differences?*
- How effective are the candidate's interpersonal and conflict resolution skills?

As you can readily see, interview success can well be determined by how well you can address these questions.

INTERVIEW STRATEGY

The first rule in planning your interview strategy is, "Never be overly critical of any past boss." To do so is only going to invite trouble and raise more doubts in the mind of the employer about the suitability of your candidacy. Instead, always provide a balanced view, stating first what you consider to be the boss's strengths before mentioning the differences in your relationship.

The second rule, when answering these types of questions, is to avoid attacking the boss personally. Don't use negative terms to describe the former boss, such as "a real meat head," "a total jerk," "stupid," (even if true). Instead, provide an ever-so-brief description of your differences in terms of style and/or philosophy, and then transition as quickly as possible to another more positive topic.

When explaining the reasons for this less-than-ideal relationship, never state that you "disliked" your boss. Instead, downplay the severity of the negative aspects of your relationship by simply stating that you had some "minor differences" in viewpoint or style. Such differences are both commonplace and understandable, so you don't want to overplay your hand when providing the rationale for these differences.

Whatever you do, don't dwell on your differences or over-explain them. This will only arouse further suspicion, since you are likely to come across as "too defensive" or "overly sensitive." Such behavior will only serve to heighten the employer's concerns. Instead be brief, to-the-point, and nonapologetic. Don't volunteer unnecessary information or ramble on with your answer. Let the employer ask follow-up questions if it is felt that additional information is required.

If you have had a long history of highly satisfactory relationships with other bosses you have worked under, highlight this fact. Tell the employer that, perhaps with this one exception, you have thoroughly enjoyed your working relationships with all of your past bosses. This will help to dispel any negative notion that the employer may have developed about your interpersonal effectiveness. Most interviewers will feel that one minor, isolated incident is hardly grounds for alarm.

Finally, when describing what it was that you liked about a particular boss's style or philosophy, be sensitive to the apparent management style and philosophy of the new boss with whom you would be working. You don't want to be describing, as your ideal boss, someone who represents the antithesis of the person with whom you are interviewing. This will hardly leave a warm feeling about your employment candidacy.

In fact, as part of your interview strategy, you need to find out something about the new hiring boss's style and philosophy before (or at the beginning of) the interview. Here again it would be advantageous to use your networking contacts to talk with others currently employed by the company to get a fix on the hiring boss's style prior to arriving for the interview. Failing this, should you have the opportunity to talk with someone in human resources or perhaps one of your potential peers, it is fair game to inquire about the hiring boss's philosophy and management style. Here are some basic questions you might consider using:

- *How would you describe Barbara's management style?*
- *How does she go about managing others?*
- *Confidentially, what is it like to work for Barbara?*
- *What do you particularly like about her management style?*
- *Few bosses are ideal to work for; in what areas as a boss do you feel Barbara could improve her effectiveness?*
- *Being compatible with the boss's style and philosophy is very important. How would you categorize Barbara's management style and/or philosophy?*
- *What insights can you provide concerning Barbara's management style and philosophy?*

In the event you are unable to have such an opportunity, in advance of your meeting with the future boss, you will have to rely on both your observation and basic interview skills as you interface with this individual. Early in the interview, should you have the opportunity, you may want to ask the hiring boss one or two of the following questions to gain some important early intelligence concerning this person's style:

- *Barbara, how would you describe your overall management style and philosophy? How do you go about managing others?*
- *Barbara, how do you like to work with your subordinates from a management planning and control standpoint?*
  - *—What role would I play in the planning process?*
  - *—What is your process for establishing performance standards?*
  - *—How will my performance be reviewed?*
- *What do you feel is important to establishing a good working relationship between you and your subordinates?*
- *As it relates to this position, what kind of decisions will you look to me to make, and what types of decisions would you prefer to reserve for yourself as the boss?*
- *What do you believe is important to establishing a productive working relationship with those who report to you?*

CLASSIC ANSWERS

The following are offered as examples of effective ways to answer many of the interview questions you may encounter concerning relationships with your boss:

I have always had a good relationship with my boss, so I find it difficult to pick the boss I liked least. If I had to make a choice, however, I would have to pick Walt Meyers. Walt's a great guy and really means well, but sometimes he doesn't always think before he talks. As a result, he did not have a good relationship with his boss, Jim Dawson, our director of marketing. Consequently, we all tended to suffer a bit, especially at budget time, when Jim would make it a point to be particularly tough on Walt. Sometimes we would get arbitrary budget cuts of as much as 30 percent, which deprived us of the support we needed to get the job done well. Although I certainly got along well with Walt, I can honestly say I was glad when he elected to take early retirement. Our relationship with Jim Dawson improved quite a bit at that point.

*   *   *

Although I am quite flexible and have worked very successfully for several bosses who have had very different styles, I prefer working for someone who is demanding of high performance, and who is open and fair in his or her management style. I prefer working for someone who is supportive, but will push me to my full capability and challenge me to continually grow and learn. I think being stretched in this way is the only way you learn and grow rapidly. I enjoy this kind of challenge and stimulation.

*   *   *

Although my relationship with my boss, Jane, has been a very good one, I suppose the one area in which we have a minor difference in viewpoint is concerning the best way to implement our new Total Quality Program. I would much prefer to start by getting buy-in at the top of the business, and then cascade the effort downward. Jane would rather start with the hourly operating personnel, build some successes, and then push things up from below.

Both positions have their pluses and minuses, and we have had some spirited debate on the best approach. I recently agreed to do it Jane's way, and am quite willing to give it an honest try. She has made some good points, and perhaps it may work out well. In the meantime, we still continue to have a good working relationship and mutual respect for one another.

15

INTERVIEW QUESTIONS— PLANNING AND ORGANIZING SKILLS

KEY INTERVIEW QUESTIONS

Planning and organizing skills are the precursors to efficiency and productivity. If you want to find an efficient, productive worker, look for someone who is well-organized. Employers know this, and they often use certain interview questions to measure a candidate's planning and organizing skills.

You might have to face the following representative questions on this topic during the course of the employment interview:

- *Describe your planning process.*
- *What is your planning schedule?*
- *How often do you do planning? Why?*
- *What are the basic steps you follow in your planning process?*

- *What do you believe about the relationship between planning and organizational success?*
- *What do you believe about the relationship between planning and individual success?*
- *Tell me about your current business plan and key objectives.*
- *When do you feel planning can get in the way of results?*
- *Tell me about your daily work routine. How do you start the day? What do you do next? What determines where you will spend your time?*
- *How and when do you go about establishing work priorities?*
- *Tell me about a time when good planning really paid off for you.*
- *Tell me about a time when you wish you had done more planning. What happened? How could it have been avoided? What did you learn from this?*

Good planning is the sign of an orderly mind, and an orderly mind is the foundation for productivity and efficiency. People who are organized in their work are the ones who do an efficient job of planning and focusing organizational resources on achieving the strategic goals of the company. They are the ones who are responsible for bringing about positive change and organizational improvement.

The key link between people and profit is the planning process. How well people plan, utilize, and control the other resources of the business (i.e., capital, raw materials, labor, equipment, technology) will determine whether or not the enterprise thrives and is profitable. The key ingredient is planning and organizing skills.

Highly successful people are generally those who are good planners. They set goals and put together the plans and steps that must be taken to achieve these goals. The plan serves to focus their activities and actions in an efficient way that keeps them focused on achieving the desired end results.

Persons with poor planning and organizing skills lack focus and direction. They tend to engage in a series of random activities that have little or no bearing to driving the organization forward and achieving the continuous change and improvement so necessary to long-term success and survival.

Employers have a strong preference for those who are efficient and orderly in their work. Planning and organizing skills are the principal foundations for such efficiency and increased productivity and, therefore, employers seek out those with these desirable skills.

INTERVIEW STRATEGY

Effective interview strategy in this category requires you to paint a picture of someone who is well-organized. You need to be able to demonstrate your proficiency in the planning area by being prepared to describe the overall planning process by which you assign priorities and organize your work.

Spend some time thinking through how you go about planning. When do you do your planning? What steps do you follow in performing the planning function, and what principles do you use to establish work priorities and set key objectives? Be prepared to clearly describe this process in some detail, and to cite some of your current work priorities and overall business objectives.

Some interview questions, as you can see from the list, will focus on your daily work routine, and how you go about organizing and planning your day. Being able to talk about your daily planning process suggests that you are efficient, well-organized, focused, purposeful, and that you are concerned with the productive use of your time.

CLASSIC ANSWERS

The following are some reasonably good answers to some of these questions about your planning and organizing skills:

Generally, I organize my work by using a combination of annual planning combined with a quarterly review process. Most of my overall planning takes place in September as part of the annual budget review process. At that time, I do a total review of each of my functional areas of responsibility with a view toward identifying improvement opportunities. For each of these functional areas, I will typically identify between four to six opportunities for improvement. I then prioritize these on the basis of what I believe are those opportunities that will most contribute to the company's strategic objectives.

At this point, I talk with my key internal customers to get their input on what they feel would be most helpful to them in accomplishing their goals and objectives.

Armed with this information, I then ask for a meeting with my boss and present my findings and recommendations to him. After some discussion, we jointly agree on what the final objectives and goals for the year will be. This is then followed by detailed planning, including the preparation of the necessary budget to support these plans and goals.

Although I review my progress against plan on a monthly basis, I do perform detailed quarterly reviews as well. Because of the dynamics of a fast-growth company such as Anderson Corporation, the quarterly reviews are also used to test the viability of the original objectives. It is not uncommon at this point to cancel one or two of the original objectives in favor of adding one or two that are now more important. This quarterly review keeps us focused on what is really important, and we need to shift our emphasis and priorities accordingly.

*   *   *

I think there is a strong relationship between planning and individual success. The planning process tends to bring some structure and order to what you are doing. Without a solid plan, you lack direction and would have a tendency to be activity rather than results-oriented. Planning brings order to the chaos around you, getting you focused on achieving the results that are going to be important to the organization. Achieving these results through orderly planning and execution of your work is what sets high-performing and successful employees apart from those who lack organization and focus. I can't imagine anyone being successful without also being good at planning.

* * *

My current business plan is focused on achieving three major objectives this year. The overall goal for the year is a 30 percent reduction in department operating costs. The plan calls for three distinct phases. These are:

1. *Reengineer the department to eliminate all nonessential, nonvalue-adding work, and to identify the key strategic work to be retained. The goal for this phase is a 25 percent reduction in total department workload—to be completed by April 1st.*
2. *Complete a department reorganization to accomplish a 40 percent staff reduction and the alignment of the best available talent against the remaining work. This is scheduled for completion by July 1st.*
3. *Identify and negotiate a financially favorable contract with an outside resource to whom we can outsource the repetitive, nonvalue-adding work considered essential to operating success. This plus the 40 percent staffing reduction are to be in place by September 30th.*

So far, we are right on target with both the objectives and deadline dates. I fully expect that we will achieve all of our objectives on time, and that we will achieve our goal of 30 percent reduction in department operating expenses.

Although these are my key objectives for the year, I am committed to accomplishing another five or six less critical objectives by end of the year.

16

INTERVIEW QUESTIONS—

BUSINESS PHILOSOPHY

KEY INTERVIEW QUESTIONS

What a candidate believes is important to business success is often indicative of the business philosophy by which he or she operates. Particularly when interviewing management candidates, employers are often interested in understanding the candidate's overall business philosophy as the basis for determining whether or not it is consistent with the overall business philosophy of the firm.

As a management candidate, the following are typical of interview questions you are likely to encounter as the employer seeks to understand your basic business philosophy:

- *How would you describe your overall business philosophy?*

- *What are three examples of things you do in your daily operations that reflect your basic business beliefs?*
- *What do you feel is essential to creating a successful business environment?*
- *What do you feel are sound principles for operating a successful business?*
- *What values do you feel are important to sustaining a successful business in the long run?*
- *If you were to structure a set of basic values and beliefs upon which to build a successful business, what would be included?*
- *What types of values and beliefs do you feel are detrimental to the operation of a successful business?*
- *In your judgment, why are certain businesses successful when others are not?*
- *In your opinion, what factors account for most business failures?*
- *In order to create the ideal business environment, what kinds of behaviors would you encourage and reward? Why?*
- *What types of behaviors would you discourage or even penalize?*
- *What do you believe are universal characteristics of successful organizations? What are the guiding principles of those organizations?*
- *Are there universal characteristics of organizations that fail? What are they? What errors do these organizations make?*
- *How have you used some of your basic business principles and beliefs to realize some key accomplishments?*
- *How do successful business organizations manage their employees? Contrast this with unsuccessful businesses.*
- *How do successful businesses go about planning and allocating their resources? Contrast this with less successful organizations.*

- *Describe the planning and decision-making processes that are important to successful business operations.*
- *What do you believe is characteristic of the planning and decision-making processes of unsuccessful enterprises? What is missing?*
- *What kind of behaviors do highly successful organizations encourage and reward? Why?*
- *What kinds of behaviors do less successful companies encourage and reward? Why is this a detriment to success?*

Over the years, most companies develop a distinct business or operating philosophy that guides organizational behavior and decision making. This is sometimes referred to as the company's "value or belief system." It is what the company believes to be important to the organization's success, and it permeates and guides much of how the organization behaves with respect to its various business processes—how it goes about planning, how it allocates resources, how it manages and rewards its employees.

Some organizations, like Johnson & Johnson, have formalized this philosophy in the form of a credo, which is supported by a written set of beliefs and operating principles that are intended to keep management and employees focused on what the organization believes is important to its success. Other organizations have not gone to this extent to formalize their beliefs, but nonetheless, a basic core value system *does* exist!

As organizations consider employment candidates, it is common practice to ask some questions concerning the individual's business philosophy—what the candidate feels is important to business or organizational success. This is done to assure the organization that they will be hiring someone who is compatible with and will support the company's overall business philosophy.

I was recently hired as a consultant by a major, multi-billion dollar oil company to design a set of interview questions that would help them to more consistently select and hire persons who were compatible with their core business beliefs and philosophy (which were formalized in a written brochure distributed to its management and employees).

More and more companies are beginning to take this matter of business philosophy seriously. Many are now, if they haven't already done so, publishing their philosophy and using it as the basis for both employee selection and development. You are bound to see more and more questions of this type in the employment interview. You will therefore need to be prepared to answer them.

INTERVIEW STRATEGY

Business philosophy is one of those selection criteria that is again going to vary from employer to employer. Although I believe there are some fairly universal criteria now emerging that have become popularized by current business trends (i.e, employee participation, the team concept, reengineering, total quality, and the like), you can by no means count on using one single interview strategy with all employers, if you wish to come out on the winning side of the equation.

Here again, we are faced with the need to understand the employer's preferences in advance (or at the beginning) of the employment interview. If, as in the case of Johnson & Johnson, the employer has a written credo or statement of guiding principles and beliefs (and many now do), it would be an excellent idea to get a copy of these in advance. Many times they are available through the employment department (or the employment agency) just for the asking. Having a copy of this document to study in advance is sure to provide you with a huge competitive advantage in the interview.

In the absence of a written business philosophy, you will need to get a little more creative in scheming to get this important information in advance of the interview day. Here is where some good networking skills can come in handy. By calling acquaintances or members of your professional association currently employed by your target company, it may be possible to network to them in an effort to get some "inside intelligence" about the company's overall business philosophy and value system. Most will be more than willing to share their observations with you. This certainly beats going into the interview "cold," with no idea of what is important to the organization.

In the absence of such networking contacts and in the absence of being able to acquire a written document detailing the company's philosophy and beliefs, things get a little more dicey. Now you have to rely on your guile and cunning to ferret this kind of information out early in the interview discussion. To do so will require asking some fundamental questions as early as possible in the interview discussion. Here are some you might try:

- *How would you describe the general business philosophy of the Carter Company? What does the company believe is important to its business success?*
- *If you had to categorize the fundamental principles and beliefs by which the company operates, what do you feel they are?*
- *What basic principles do you feel the Carter Company believes are fundamental to its overall success?*

Answers to these questions early in the interview should prove quite helpful in understanding what is important to the company, and how you will need to package yourself to fit the preferred profile. By stating and reinforcing your belief in similar principles throughout the interview discussion, you will provide the employer with a "warm feeling" about your compatibility with the core business philosophy of the company, and create the feeling that you would fit in quite nicely.

If all else fails, and you are unsuccessful (either before or early in the interview) in gaining insight about the organization's core belief and value system, then you will be shooting in the dark. In the absence of such helpful information, as part of your strategy, you may want to hang your hat on what appears to be the new, emerging business philosophy which so many firms are now flocking to. By doing so, the odds are likely to increase in your favor.

Called by various names (e.g., team environment, high-performance work system, technician system, participative management), this new, emerging, and highly-popular business environment is categorized by:

- Flatter, leaner organizations.
- Elimination of many (if not most) middle management positions.
- Delegation of decision making to the lowest organizational level.
- Emphasis on team versus individual decision making.
- Doing more with fewer people and resources.
- Reengineering approach (reinventing the way work is done).
- Emphasis on continuous improvement.
- Strong customer focus (goal is total customer satisfaction).
- Emphasis on total quality (doing it right the first time).
- Changed role for management:
  —Provide strategic direction and leadership to the organization.
  —Provide support and act as a resource to people doing the work.
  —Provide resources to support work objectives.
  —Act as coach, counselor, teacher, facilitator, and enabler of others.

The interview implications of this new, emerging work culture should be fairly obvious. When answering questions concerning business philosophy and what is needed for organizational success, one will want to key into the above described profile.

Individual professionals, therefore, when asked about the basic principles that are important to organization success will want to talk about the importance of team versus individual decision making, the value of team membership, the need to pursue continuous improvement, the importance of satisfying the customer, the value of the total quality approach, and so on.

On the other hand, managerial candidates, when asked about their business philosophy in the interview, will want to talk about the importance of the participative approach to management as a means of bringing about significant organization improvement and success. They will also want to talk about the importance of management's providing only strategic leadership and direction to the organization, but leaving the day-to-day decision making to the work teams and individuals actually responsible for doing the work. Managerial candidates should further describe their leadership role as that of acting as a resource to the teams, providing them with the resources and support needed to get the job done. In describing what is required for organization success, it is also advisable for these candidates to talk about the importance of both the continuous improvement and total quality approaches as important to both short- and long-term success.

Although there is no absolute guarantee, the odds are greatly in your favor that describing and expounding on your belief in the above business principles and general philosophy will be a winning combination in today's modern business climate. In the absence of advance intelligence and specific knowledge of the employer's actual business philosophy, I would recommend the pursuit of the "participative management" approach to describing your business philosophy. However, whenever it is possible to do so, eliminate this somewhat risky guessing game in favor of first-hand information about the firm's actual core values and beliefs.

CLASSIC ANSWERS

As already discussed, there is no one, single "right" answer to the interview questions you may be asked with regard to business philosophy. Whether or not a particular answer is "right" will depend entirely upon the individual philosophy and beliefs of the organization with which you will be interviewing. Ideally, to be victorious in the interview, you must tailor your answers to what is important to that firm.

Assuming such compatibility, the following represent some good examples of the way that the topic of business philosophy might be addressed in the employment interview:

My business philosophy is one that believes in the importance of tapping the full human potential of the organization. I am a strong advocate of the participative approach to management. Since people plan and manage all of the resources of the business (such as capital, raw materials, equipment, technology, etc.), the ability to develop and motivate people to effectively control these resources is paramount to achieving profitability and organizational success.

To achieve organizational success, therefore, I think it important to develop the core skills and competencies of your people and then drive day-to-day decision making to the lowest level of the organization possible. This motivates and empowers people to bring about the major improvements required for organizational success.

* * *

I think successful firms have always understood what is today called the "total quality" approach to management. Deming and some of the other modern-day gurus have simply applied statistics to what have always been basic success principles. "Achieving total customer satisfaction" is critical to maintaining your competitive advantage, and always has been. "Doing it right the first time" assures customer satisfaction, eliminates defects and returns, eliminates waste, and eliminates the unnecessary staff required to deal with all these problems. Companies who live by this philosophy have an enormous cost and market advantage over their competition. I think total quality is the basis for success of today's modern company.

* * *

I believe that organizational success has a lot to do with the role that management plays in providing strategic leadership and unleashing the potential of its employees through the team approach. Organizations that are not successful have yet to learn this important lesson. In these companies, management sees its role as that of the key decision maker with the role of the employees being to carry out the decisions of management. Employees are treated as if they are incapable of thought. The result is that they stop thinking and begin to function as mindless robots. Since they are not paid to think, they don't think. The net result is mindless, nonthinking workers making our products. This results in lack of pride in workmanship, poor product quality, dissatisfied customers, waste, higher manufacturing and material costs, and so on. The list goes on and on. The bottom line of such philosophy is eventual business failure.

Successful organizations, on the other hand, are those that develop their employees' capabilities, and who motivate and empower them to make the decisions necessary to continuously improve both product and processes. These are the organizations that are the real success stories in today's highly competitive business environment. The others will end up on the dust heaps of history.

17

INTERVIEW QUESTIONS— OPERATING STYLE

KEY INTERVIEW QUESTIONS

Operating style has to do with the way you operate or performs your work. It is a reflection of the way in which you plan, execute, and control the quality of your work. Operating style is a measurement of your work habits, and is usually a reflection of some broader operating principles and beliefs that you believe are important to your personal performance and success.

The following array of questions may be encountered in the interview as the prospective employer attempts to get a handle on how you go about carrying out your job responsibilities:

- *How would you describe your operating style—the way you go about getting your work done?*

- *What do you believe are the day-to-day operating principles that are important to personal success?*
- *How is the way you approach your work different from others in your group?*
- *In what way is your work style unique?*
- *What benefits do you derive through using this operating style?*
- *What type of work style do you believe is important to good performance?*
- *What are the underlying principles and beliefs you feel are important to an effective operating style and good performance?*
- *What kind of operating style do you believe is characteristic of poor performers?*
- *What do you believe are the key differences in operating style between good performers and poor performers?*
- *What are the basic work principles by which you operate?*
- *Why are these work principles important to you?*
- *How are some of your basic work principles reflected in one or two of your key accomplishments?*
- *Cite some examples of how some of your basic work principles and operating style have aided your performance.*
  —What principles did you employ?
  —What performance benefits were realized?
- *Give me an example where you abandoned one of your fundamental work principles, and how it affected your performance.*
  —What basic principle did you abandon?
  —How did it impact your performance?
  —What learning resulted from this experience?
- *What do you believe are the key operating or work principles by which most successful people operate?*
- *How do these principles translate into success?*

- *What key operating or work principles are most frequently ignored by poor performers?*
- *If your co-workers were asked to describe your operating style and work habits, what do you think they would say?*
- *What aspects of your work style would they say are particularly good?*
- *What improvements might they suggest in your operating style?*
- *How does your personal philosophy affect the way you perform your work?*
- *How would your boss describe or categorize your work style?*

Operating style is the process by which one plans, organizes, and carries out his or her work. Persons who have productive work styles are usually well-organized and tend to have a systematic way of approaching their work. The work habits or operating style of effective people normally include the following steps or phases:

Assessment Phase

During this phase, the person steps back and takes a broad, strategic look at his or her job responsibilities for the purpose of identifying opportunities for improvement. This includes opportunities for improved efficiency in existing work processes (i.e., doing work differently) as well as new opportunities for performance improvement.

Goal Setting Phase

Almost all successful people are known to set and work toward specific goals. During this phase, the individual reviews the various opportunities for improvement identified during the assessment phase and assigns priorities and specific goals. Intelligent workers will normally get input and buy-in from the boss at this point, knowing full well that success will require management support and the commitment of the needed resources required to attain the goals.

Analysis

Once goals are set, the next step is detailed analysis. This normally includes a thorough definition of the problem(s) to be solved as well as analysis of the variables affecting the problem(s) and their cause-and-effect relationships.

Planning

During the planning phase, a step-by-step plan of attack is formulated, and specific time tables are established for each. This includes planning and scheduling of the resources needed to carry out the plan.

Execution

This is the phase during which the plan is carried out and the work is actually performed. It entails carrying out the steps of the plan in a systematic way so as to meet the various timetables and benchmarks established during the planning step.

Evaluation and Feedback

This is the final phase during which the individual assesses and evaluates the effectiveness of the plan. This normally includes feedback from others, particularly customers (internal and external) who are the intended beneficiaries of the work. Opportunities are then identified for further improvement.

When looking for productive persons with good work habits and a solid operating style, employers will normally seek candidates who are organized and systematic in how they approach their work. They will, therefore, expect to hear successful candidates describe an orderly approach to their work that includes the various phases of the work process as just delineated. There will also be a tendency to look for individuals who are self-motivated and who have a strong drive for continuous improvement.

INTERVIEW STRATEGY

In this age of reengineered, downsized organizations, most managers are under great pressure to produce more, better, and with fewer resources. This includes fewer people. An employment candidate with strong operating style reflecting good work habits, effective organization, good planning, solid execution, attainment of timely results, and satisfied customers (internal and external) is bound to give most hiring managers a very warm feeling.

When asked about your operating or work style by the employer during the interview, therefore, an effective strategy would be to key off the steps of the work process just outlined. You want to come across as focused, hard-working, a planner, organized, thorough at execution, timely, and results-oriented. You should also demonstrate that you are self-motivated, pursue continuous improvement, and are committed to achieving the total satisfaction of those whom you serve (i.e., boss and customers). In almost all cases, this should prove to be a winning combination!

CLASSIC ANSWERS

The following answers should serve as reliable models for planning your own answers to interview questions that are intended to evaluate your operating style:

My operating style can best be described as focused, well-organized, and strongly committed to bringing about improvement in the functional areas for which I am responsible.

I tend to take a project approach to carrying out my work. This includes defining opportunities for improvement, setting specific goals, formulating a workable plan, carrying out the plan in a timely fashion, and assessing results. I like to include my internal customers in the planning process and, where possible, partner with them in bringing about the improvement.

Since my overall operating goal is customer satisfaction, I feel it is important to get them involved in any way that I can. I suppose the best evidence I have of the effectiveness of this approach are the several complimentary letters from satisfied customers that are in my personnel file.

* * *

I believe the operating styles of poor performers probably reflect, in large measure, a lack of good planning and focus. Poor performers, I believe wait for things to happen, and then react to them. Good performers, on the other hand, are persons who plan to make things happen, and are continuously motivated to achieve improved results. Setting goals, planning, good execution, and timely follow-through, I think are the basic operating principles underlying good performance.

* * *

Although certainly not a key problem, I believe I could improve my work performance by taking time to do more planning. Although by nature I believe in the importance of planning to achieve successful performance, like most people, however, I sometimes get so caught up in the day-to-day operating demands of the job that I can't seem to find the time to do some of the strategic planning I know could be beneficial. I'm getting better at this, however. Last week, I went off-site for three hours to do some strategic planning. As a result, I now have some longer term goals for my function and a specific plan to achieve them. I think this is a good starting point.

18

INTERVIEW QUESTIONS— COMMUNICATIONS SKILLS

KEY INTERVIEW QUESTIONS

How effective are you at communications? How well can you get your point across to others? Can you do so in a concise, crisp way without rambling along and losing the interest of your audience? These are all points the employer is going to be looking at in the evaluation of your verbal and written communications skills.

Since employers are getting a living, real time demonstration of your verbal skills as the interview progresses, there is not much need for them to ask you very many questions about this area. However, the interviewer is likely to inquire about your writing skills, if these are important to the position for which you are being interviewed.

Should the employer elect to "check you out" in the communications area, you may encounter one or more of the following questions during the course of the employment interview:

- *On a scale of 1 to 10 (10 = outstanding, 5 = average, 1 = poor), where would you rate your overall communications skills? Why?*
- *Using the same scale, where would you rate your verbal communication skills? Why?*
- *Likewise, on the same scales. how would you rank your written communication skills? Why?*
- *What evidence can you provide that documents the effectiveness of your overall communications skills?*
- *Give me an example of something complex that you needed to effectively communicate to others.*
  —What made it complex?
  —Why was it difficult to communicate?
  —What did you do to communicate effectively?
  —What were the results?
  —How might these results have been improved?
- *What evidence can you provide of the effectiveness of your written communication skills?*
- *How well do you write?*

The ability to communicate effectively with others has always been a valued skill with most employers. Today, with the crush of time and enormous pressures of overwhelming workloads, the need for effective communications skills is paramount. We are in the midst of the information explosion, and the information superhighway is all but paved and ready to go.

Although the need to communicate has increased significantly, as more and more information comes to us faster and faster, the time allotted for person-to-person direct communication has become increasingly shortened. Technology has filled the gap with the advent of voice mail and E-mail, and other innovations will soon be arriving. With the shorter windows for direct communications and the growth of electronic communications in various forms has come the need for far more succinct, concise, and effective verbal and written communication skills.

With these rapid changes, employers are looking for people who are multi-faceted in their ability to communicate effectively in both written and verbal form. Being able to demonstrate these skills effectively in the interview could prove an important factor in your selection as the favored candidate for the position being offered.

INTERVIEW STRATEGY

Your verbal communication skills (or lack thereof) are going to be rather evident throughout the interview. It is important, therefore, that you are attentive to them. Here are some basic guidelines to follow in communicating effectively:

1. Be expressive. Use alive, animated speech. Avoid using a monotone.
2. Be conscious of your articulation. Pronounce words clearly. Don't mumble or slur your speech.
3. Be concise. Avoid being too wordy or rambling.
4. Stay focused and to the point.
5. Be direct and forthright. Don't be evasive or beat around the bush.
6. Use appropriate hand gestures to emphasize key points. Avoid overuse of the hands.

Using this book to practice answering interview questions should help to fine-tune your answers and improve your verbal communication skills. Take advantage of this opportunity to practice.

Should you know in advance that the position is going to require extensive use of written communications skills (e.g., a job in public affairs, technical writing, writing advertising copy), it would be advisable to take samples of your writing along with you to the interview. In this way, if you are asked about these skills, you can produce these sample documents for the interviewer to see.

CLASSIC ANSWERS

Here are some classic answers that might be used as models for formulating your interview strategy in this interview set:

> *On a scale of 1 to 10, 10 being excellent, I would rate my written communication skills at either the "9" or the "10" level. The best evidence that I can offer of my skills in this area is the fact that I was an associate editor of our college newspaper. I also earned an "A" in Freshman Composition. I have always had strong writing skills.*
>
> *Using the same scale, I would also rank my verbal skills quite high. Earlier in my career, I served as a trainer for our field sales group, and ran hundreds of sales training seminars. Course evaluation sheets from the participants consistently ranked my training and communication skills at the "9" or "10" level.*

*   *   *

> *Writing has always been a strength. This seems to be well known among co-workers since they always seek me out for ideas or critique when they have something difficult to write.*

*   *   *

> *The most difficult communications challenge I have faced was to effectively communicate the changes in benefit coverage as we converted from a standard, one-size-fits-all benefit program to a cafeteria-style benefits plan. These changes needed to be communicated to over 20,000 employees.*
>
> *The overall communications strategy was quite elaborate and involved a multimedia approach using a combination of brochures, mass meetings with slide presentations, and E-mail. Despite the enormity of the challenge, things came off without a hitch.*

19

INTERVIEW QUESTIONS— MANAGEMENT STYLE

KEY INTERVIEW QUESTIONS

In the modern organization, the number of management positions is decreasing as many companies eliminate millions of middle-management positions in favor of flatter and leaner organizational structures. Additionally, with the fast-moving trend toward the team environment coupled with the efforts to move day-to-day decision making to the lowest possible rungs of the organizational ladder, the fundamental role and mission of management has shifted dramatically. So has the management profile sought by most companies.

All of this translates into far stiffer competition for fewer management positions, combined with tougher employment interviews and tighter selection standards for management candidates. The bottom line is that such candidates can now expect a far more intense grilling during the interview process than in the past. As a result, the following is a good, representative sampling of questions that the management candidate can now expect to encounter in the employment interview:

- *What do you believe to be the characteristics of an effective manager?*
  - *—Which are the most important attributes?*
  - *—Why are they important?*
- *How would you describe your management philosophy?*
- *Describe your management process—the process by which you manage others.*
- *With which of the following two management styles do you most closely identify, and why?*
  - *—Controlling: Like to make most decisions personally and have subordinates carry out specific directions.*
  - *—Participative: Like to involve others in the decision-making process as much as possible, and provide only broad, strategic direction to subordinates.*
- *How would your subordinates describe your management style?*
  - *—In what areas would they be complimentary?*
  - *—In what areas would they suggest improvement?*
- *What has your boss said about your management effectiveness during performance reviews?*
  - *—What does he or she consider to be your management strengths?*
  - *—What areas have been suggested for improvement?*
- *What do you feel are your strongest attributes as a manager?*
- *How could you improve your managerial effectiveness?*
- *What is the proper role of a manager? Why?*
- *What is the difference between a manager and a leader?*
- *Are you more of a manager or more of a leader? Explain your answer.*

- *Describe your planning process as a manager.*
- *What techniques do you use to motivate poor performers?*

  —*Give me some real-life examples.*

  —*What results did you get?*

  —*How could these results have been improved?*

- *What is the toughest management decision you have had to make?*

  —*Why was it tough?*

  —*What decision did you make?*

  —*What was the outcome?*

- *Describe how you evaluate subordinate performance.*

  —*What basis is used for evaluation?*

  —*What standards are used?*

  —*How do you measure performance against these standards?*

  —*How do you communicate this performance?*

- *Describe how you monitor and control department operations.*

  —*What performance benchmarks do you use?*

  —*How do you monitor against these benchmarks?*

  —*What controls do you exercise?*

  —*How effective is this process? Why?*

  —*How could this process be improved?*

- *Describe your approach to employee development.*

  —*How do you determine development needs?*

  —*How are these communicated?*

  —*How is accountability assigned?*

  —*What successes have you had?*

  —*How could this process be improved?*

- *Describe your employee selection process.*

  —*How do you define candidate qualifications?*

  —*What is your approach to interviewing?*

  —*How do you go about final candidate selection?*

—What evidence can you cite for selection effectiveness?

—How could you improve this process?

- *What measurable, tangible evidence can you provide of your managerial effectiveness?*
- *How could you improve your managerial effectiveness?*
- *Why do you believe that you are an effective manager?*

Managerial style goes hand-in-hand with organizational culture. If the work environment is a tough, hard-nosed, get-it-done culture that has little regard for employee development and is focused on the management of "things" rather than "people," then the preferred management profile will follow suit. Such an organization will likely favor managers who are highly controlling by nature. They will prefer candidates who are "hard-nosed, decisive, aggressive, get-it-done-at-all-cost" types who will call all the shots and expect employees to jump through hoops to get it done exactly as told.

On the other hand, if the organization subscribes to the new, modern, participative management culture, the preferred candidate profile is going to be considerably different. In this case, the company will be in search of managers who are strongly committed to employee involvement, and who believe that the success of organizations requires that employees have a major stake in the decision-making process.

These employers will seek candidates who believe their role, as a manager, is to be the "visionary"—the one responsible for creating the vision of what is possible to achieve, thus providing the strategic goals and direction to the work team. Under this management philosophy, it is the work team's role, then, to decide how to best achieve the vision and for "making it happen."

Such employers will quickly screen out controlling style managers in favor of candidates who see their principal operating role as that of serving as a resource to the work group—to provide the team with what is required in the way of resources and support needed to actualize the vision and turn it into a reality. Successful candidates, in this case, would describe their role as being a "visionary, strategic leader, coach, counselor, cheerleader, teacher, facilitator, and enabler of others." Such a manager believes that organization success is achieved through the management of "people," not the management of "things."

Regardless of organizational climate and preferred management style, you can bet on one thing—as a management candidate you are probably in for a pretty thorough probing during the interview. With the growing scarcity of management positions and a plethora of exceptionally well-qualified candidates from which to choose, organizations are going to be just that—"choosy." So you will need to hone your interviewing skills to a fine, sharp edge if you want to get a leg up over some pretty steep competition.

INTERVIEW STRATEGY

At the risk of sounding like a broken record, management style is one of those selection criteria that is unique to the work environment of the company with whom you are interviewing. There is no "one-size-fits-all" strategy for answering this barrage of potential interview questions regarding your management style. What is the "right" answer for one organization is bound to be the "wrong" answer for the next.

Unless you are just plain lucky, developing a winning strategy will depend upon your assessing the nature of the work environment in advance of (or early in) the interview. By asking the right questions of networking contacts currently employed with your target firm, or through use of some skillful interview questions strategically placed in the early stages of the interview, you can systematically collect the kind of information about the work environment and culture needed to formulate an effective interview strategy.

Here are some questions that should prove particularly helpful:

- *What can you tell me about the management style and philosophy of the Walton Corporation?*
- *How would you characterize the predominant management style found at Walton Corporation?*

- *What type of management philosophy and style is required for success at Walton Corporation?*
- *How would you describe the predominant management beliefs and philosophy by which Walton Corporation's managers operate?*
- *How would you characterize what most Walton managers believe is most important to successful business operations?*

Answers to these and similar questions should provide you with valuable insight concerning the type of management profile the employer is seeking. Networking through personal contacts (or your professional association members) now employed at the target company, in advance of the interview, would be particularly advantageous since you will have time to fine-tune your strategy and specific answers to this set of interview questions. This should allow you the luxury of sharpening your answers considerably.

In the absence of such valuable contacts, you will need to use your interview skills to acquire this information during the interview itself. In this case, it is suggested that you ask one or more of the above questions early in the interview discussion so that you will have sufficient time to digest the answers and formulate an appropriate strategy for answering management style questions.

In the event that the interview structure precludes this kind of opportunity, you are left to guess at what the management culture and style of the employer is like. Be particularly alert and observant, therefore, to how the managers with whom you have contact behave, and how they seem to relate to their subordinates. Through some careful observations, you can probably come up with some pretty strong clues concerning the overall management philosophy and style of the company.

If all else fails, I suggest that you assume that the preferred management style is one based on the concepts of employee empowerment, team-based decision making, and a participative management style. The current management trend is moving so heavily in this direction today that your odds of being right are probably far greater than 50 percent.

Whatever your tack, a successful interview strategy will surely require that you describe your management philosophy and style such that it is congruous with predominant profile of the target firm's current management team. Understanding what they believe and value as important to successful business management is critical to the success of such a strategy.

CLASSIC ANSWERS

As I have repeatedly emphasized, there is no absolute "right" answer to the questions on management style that will work for all interviews with all employers. If your goal is to be successful in the interview, each answer will need to be tailored to the management culture of the organization with which you will be interviewing.

The following answers are therefore simply intended to stimulate your thinking, and to provide a basic framework for developing your own answers to this interview set:

I am a strong advocate of participative management. My management style is based upon the belief that for any business to succeed and realize its full potential, it must make use of its full human resource capability. I see my greatest responsibility being to develop and motivate my people to achieve the strategic goals of the organization. By organizing my team around the goals and giving them the support and resources they need, my experience has shown that time and time again they will achieve or exceed expectations.

* * *

I think what my subordinates would tell you they most like about my management style is my tendency to get out of their way when they have something important to do. All kidding aside, I am a firm believer in the power of team management and employee empowerment. I've seen it work, and it's a powerful tool! I believe my job, as a manager, is to point the way, provide the resources and encouragement, and then stand back and get out of the way.

It is surprising what empowered work teams can do if you only give them the chance. For example, during the start-up of our new finishing line, I managed an empowered work team, which included future hourly operators, to both plan and start up the manufacturing line. Astoundingly, we beat projected start-up date by a full month and were running at machine design capacity within eight months. As you know this is almost unheard of!

*   *   *

My management planning process is extremely team-oriented. During the initial planning phase, I hold a series of team meetings with my group to get their ideas and recommendations about key opportunities for improvement. I then facilitate group meetings for the purpose of selecting the most promising opportunities. We then, as a group, establish specific goals, priorities, and assign accountability. The team members then have the responsibility to do the detailed planning and determine how they are going to accomplish the objectives. These plans then become the basis for our daily operation, and the benchmarks by which we gauge our progress.

*   *   *

As with most managers, the toughest decision I have had to make was to fire someone I liked and who was trying his darndest to bring his performance up to standard. Despite a performance improvement plan and some real efforts at training and development, we determined that the job was simply beyond his capability, and we arrived at the decision to let him go. Fortunately, it had a good ending since, with our help, he was able to land a job as an analyst with Cooper Bank and is doing quite well. I know he's much happier in this job, and he still stays in touch and stops by occasionally to say hello.

*   *   *

Although I feel that I am a reasonably good manager, and I think my subordinates would agree with that assessment, the one area in which I believe there is room for some improvement is my knowledge of financial analysis. Although I have strong mathematical and accounting skills, I am still occasionally baffled by some of the financial planning models used by our analysts. I've resolved to do something about this, however, and have enrolled in a financial analysis course for non-finance majors at Baxter College for the fall term. I'm looking forward to being a little less baffled.

20

INTERVIEW QUESTIONS— CREATIVITY

KEY INTERVIEW QUESTIONS

Today with the emphasis on trends such as reengineering and continuous improvement, employers are placing a premium on creativity. For the most part, they want employees who can "think out of the box." Although difficult to measure in the interview setting, you may find employers using questions similar to the following in an effort to measure your level of creativity:

- *What are the various approaches that could be used to solve the following problem (employer cites problem)?*

   —How many different approaches can you think of?

   —What would be the most creative approach to optimize results?

- *Tell me about something very creative you did.*

—What was unique about it?

—How did you arrive at the idea?

—What other possibilities did you consider?

—Why was this a particularly creative solution?

- *What examples can you give that highlight your creativity?*
- *What is the most creative thing you have done?*
- *What is the second most creative thing you have done?*
- *Do you consider yourself to be more analytical or more creative? Explain by providing some examples of things you have done.*
- *If you were at the top of a 40-story building and had to get to the rooftop of an adjacent building without going down the stairs to the street, how many ways can you think of to accomplish this?*

In the new era of corporate downsizing where the pressure is on both management and employees to do more, better, and with less, human creativity is taking on added significance in the employment interview. The new, emerging corporate culture of most modern organizations demands that individuals be highly creative in their approach to their jobs.

The major corporate push that we are now seeing through reengineering is challenging managers and employees alike to totally rethink the way work is done. These individuals are being asked to think of creative ways to eliminate unnecessary work, consolidate and streamline existing work processes, and develop totally new ways to get the same or better results with far fewer resources.

At the same time, the major shift of many organizations to concepts such as employee empowerment, high-performance work systems, sociotechnical systems, team decision making, and so on is moving the decision-making processes further and further down into the organizations. This is requiring employees to be increasingly more analytical and creative in their approaches to work as they pursue the common objective of "continuous improvement."

Today, most companies do not want to hire people who are status quo oriented. For the most part, they are not interested in hiring persons who want to do routine, repetitive work. This is the kind of work that best lends itself to computers and automation. Instead, they are interested in hiring individuals who want to pursue change and improvement, continuously looking for new and better ways to get the same or an improved result. These are the persons who are motivated to challenge the old ways of doing things in search of something better. As never before, more and more employees at all organizational levels are being asked to be increasingly creative and imaginative in how they approach their work.

Creativity, as a desirable candidate qualification, has truly come of age. More and more it is beginning to increase in importance as a criterion for employment selection. As a result, you can expect to encounter an increasing number of interview questions having to do with this subject.

INTERVIEW STRATEGY

Thinking about how to best answer questions about creativity during the employment interview is going to require some creativity on your part. (Excuse the pun!) Actually, it is going to probably require more analytical skill than true creativity.

The best way to prepare for these kinds of questions is to systematically review each of the positions you have held over the years to uncover those cases where you have used creativity as a means to achieve key results. Here is a basic process that you might try to facilitate this undertaking:

1. Make a list of each position you have held during your career.
2. For each position, try to cite at least three or four key accomplishments or results that you achieved.
3. For each accomplishment, list the various problems that you were required to solve to achieve that result.

4. Which of these involved creative or unique solutions?

5. Take a few moments to describe in writing these unique or creative approaches and the benefit realized from them.

Sometimes people have difficulty thinking of major accomplishments they achieved. One technique that I have found helpful to get their creative juices flowing has been to ask them to think about the following questions:

- *What were the major problems you faced when you first came into the job?*
- *What did you do about them?*
- *What was the result of the actions taken?*

And, now I suppose we can add, "Which of these required unique or creative thinking?"

You will find that forcing yourself to think about how you have constructively used creativity to bring about improvements to past organizations will serve as excellent advance preparation for the interview. This will not only enable you to speak convincingly about your creative ability, but you will be able to cite specific examples of how you used this creativity to achieve important results and improvements. This should prove a highly effective strategy for addressing this issue of creativity.

CLASSIC ANSWERS

Hopefully, the following examples will prove helpful to you in seeing how this category of interview questions might be effectively answered:

Perhaps one of the more creative things that I have done had to do with reducing our hiring costs by greater than 30 percent through the use of direct mail as a replacement for newspaper advertising. I remembered from a college advertising course that direct mail, if well-designed, will normally produce between a 3 percent to 5 percent favorable return rate. On the other hand, since we were recruiting research scientists with very narrow specialties, newspaper advertising was proving very ineffective, and we were paying huge advertising bills to boot.

When you ran an ad for these scientists, you really had to ask yourself the following questions. "What is the probability that a scientist with these specific credentials is going to be reading this newspaper on this particular date, turn to this specific page, see this particular ad, and at the same time have an interest in this specific position at this particular location?" When asking this question of myself, I had to admit that the probabilities were remote!

As I thought about this, it occurred to me that by using direct mail I could reach a highly targeted group of qualified individuals and would not have to depend upon the random possibility that they would see the ad I had been running. By using a computerized patent database to identify creative persons having patents in our areas of interest, I was able to design highly pinpointed direct mail campaigns to find these hard-to-find scientists.

The results were that we reduced recruiting time by 80 percent with a corresponding drop of 30 percent in advertising expense. This has saved the company almost $0.5 million annually, and has also improved the caliber of the persons we are now hiring for these positions.

*   *   *

Actually, I don't believe that you can be creative without being analytical. I believe that I am both creative and analytical. In creativity, you use a combination of abstract thinking (envisioning a barrage of possibilities) along with inductive reasoning. Once a number of varied possibilities are floating around in your head, you begin the analytical process of systematically testing each to get down to a core group of possibilities that has some merit. At this point, through experimentation,

*these possibilities can be tested for their practical appli-
cation and arrival at a final decision. Such experimental design requires analytical thinking. I am a person
who is good at coming up with the possibilities as well
as analyzing them for their practical value, and I enjoy
both activities.*

21

INTERVIEW QUESTIONS— ENTREPRENEURSHIP (RISK TAKING)

KEY INTERVIEW QUESTIONS

Because of the need for the modern organization to continuously drive for improvement as a means to assure competitiveness and survival in the marketplace, employers are beginning more and more to seek individuals who have an entrepreneurial spirit and who are willing to take reasonable risks. As a result, you may begin to see more job interview questions having to do with the subject of risk taking.

Here are some examples of the kinds of questions you may encounter during the course of your interview discussions:

- *What is your feeling about the importance of taking risks in today's business climate?*
- *Tell me about some business risks that you took recently.*

—*What were the risks you took?*

—*What were the results?*

- *What is the biggest business risk that you have ever taken?*

  —*What was the magnitude of the risk (the possible consequences)?*

  —*What compelled you to take the risk?*

  —*What was the outcome?*

  —*Would you do anything differently?*

- *Tell me about some risks you elected to take in order to bring certain improvements about.*

  —*What were the risks?*

  —*What improvements were you aiming for?*

  —*How did things work out?*

- *If you had to rate your willingness to take business risks on a scale of 1 to 10 (10 = extremely high, 5 = average, 1 = extremely low), what rating would you choose, and why?*

- *Give some examples of innovations that you brought about that required some risk taking on your part.*

  —*What were the innovations?*

  —*What risks did you assume?*

  —*What were the results?*

- *Do you feel it is more important to take risks or to be reliable and thorough? Why?*

- *In your opinion, what is the difference between prudent risk taking and imprudent risk taking?*

- *Do you consider yourself to be an entrepreneur? Why?*

- *What business risks have you taken that backfired on you?*

  —*What was the nature of the each risk?*

  —*What was at stake in each?*

  —*What were the consequences of your decisions?*

  —*Would you take these same risks again?*

- *In hindsight, what risk do you most regret not having taken? Why?*

  —What was the nature of this risk?

  —What were the stakes of being wrong?

  —Why did you elect not to take this risk?

  —What have you learned from this experience?

  —Would you likely make the same decision today?

In today's business climate, employers are demanding that more and more employees take reasonable risks in performing their jobs. There are several events occurring within corporate America that appear to be driving the need for increased employee willingness to be entrepreneurial and to take reasonable risks associated with the performance of their jobs.

As a result of extensive corporate-wide downsizing, in most organizations, managers and employees alike are being called upon to do more, do it faster, and do it better. Each employee is expected to be a "positive change agent," taking accountability for continuously bringing about change and improvement in the way work is being done. In some cases, employees are even being encouraged to perform their responsibilities as if they were running their own businesses. Thus, in the modern business climate, employees are expected to be change agents, entrepreneurs, and risk takers. Companies can no longer afford "custodians of the status quo," if they are to survive and prosper in an increasingly competitive marketplace.

Also, in many companies, downsizing has meant the elimination of virtually millions of middle-management positions in favor of flatter organizational structures and more employee decision making. Many decisions formerly made by these middle managers are now being delegated to the lowest levels of the organizations—where the actual work is done. Team decision making at this organizational level has, in essence, replaced middle management decision making. Coupled with this trend is a rapid movement to "employee empowerment," where the workers are now empowered to bring about the needed changes and improvements.

This shift in business philosophy has dramatically changed the role of workers. They are no longer only responsible for carrying out the specific instructions of management; instead, they are expected to think, to plan for improvement, and to carry out their improvement plans, looking to management for support and the resources needed to bring the improvements about.

Improvement, by its very nature, requires challenging the status quo—challenging the way things have always been done. Driving change, by its very nature, also requires taking risks and accepting the potential consequences of the change process. As the roles of workers and professionals change, so do the requirements that they be more entrepreneurial and more willing to take risks. The role of management is to encourage and support prudent risk taking in the interests of realizing change, increased productivity, and increased organizational effectiveness.

INTERVIEW STRATEGY

The message for the job seeker is unmistakable. From an interview strategy standpoint, employment candidates need to be able to effectively address these questions concerning risk taking and change, as they are increasingly encountered in the employment interview.

I need to caution you, however, that there are still some old-fashioned, top-down, type organizations out there that have not adopted this new change management philosophy. In these cases, most decisions are still being made at the top of the organization, with the employee's primary role being that of carrying out the directions and wishes of management. In such cases, the employer may not wish to have independent-minded risk takers as part of their organization, and may in fact intentionally screen such persons out during the interview process.

We must all make the best decisions for ourselves as to which type of organization we best fit if we are to be happy and realize our desired potential. If you don't enjoy being somewhat independent, or lack the entrepreneurial spirit and desire to take risks, you are probably going to be very unhappy in an "employee empowered" culture which values and rewards these characteristics. You are probably better off seeking an organization with a top-down management decision-making process, where you will not be expected to independently bring about change. On the other hand, if you have more of an entrepreneurial, risk-taking spirit you will likely want to seek an organization that values and promotes employee empowerment and will see these characteristics as positive attributes. The choice is yours, and you need to make it wisely.

The strategy you elect to employ in the interview, will need to be related to the type of company with which you are interviewing. To describe yourself as entrepreneurial and willing to take risks is probably not going to sit very well with a controlling management culture that prefers that all decision making be made at the senior management level. Likewise, describing yourself as someone who is a "good soldier," "is good at carrying out orders," and who "looks to management for most decision making" is simply not going to cut it with modern organizational cultures where the emphasis is on employee empowerment and decision making at the lowest possible organizational level.

To win in the interview, you are going to need to tailor your response to the type of organization with which you are interviewing. Advance knowledge of organizational culture or work environment is therefore critical to development of a successful strategy. Take time to inquire of networking contacts employed by the organization about what it is like to work there and what the predominant management style and philosophy of the organization is. Or, in the absence of such contacts, ask appropriate questions during the early stages of the interview to make an appropriate determination. Success of your interview strategy will depend upon it.

CLASSIC ANSWERS

In order to present a fuller understanding of effective answers to interview questions having to do with the subject of entrepreneurship and risk taking, I have distinguished between the two basic kinds of organizational cultures—"employee-empowered" and "controlling." It is unlikely, however, that you will get many (if any) questions about risk taking from organizations that favor a controlling style culture, since they are not really looking for risk takers.

Employee-Empowered Culture

On a scale of 1 to 10, I would rate my propensity for risk taking at about the 8 or 9 level. I believe that being creative, entrepreneurial, and willing to take reasonable risks is the only way to bring change and improvement to the organization. Continuous improvement and increased productivity require you to constantly question and challenge the way that things are being done, and it is the only way that change and improvement can come about. There is always risk associated with change, but unless you are willing to take these risks, no progress can be made. Although I don't believe in being foolhardy about the kinds of risks I'm willing to take, I am very prone to take prudent risks in the interests of progress and improvement.

Controlling Culture

I don't believe that it is the role of employees to make a lot of changes and take risks. Although I'm certainly prone to make recommendations for improvement, I believe that the responsibility for decision making, along with risk taking, really rests with management. My job, as I see it, is to carry out management's decisions to the best of my ability and to achieve the objectives established for my area of responsibility by my manager.

Employee-Empowered Culture

The biggest single risk that I took that backfired on me was the time I decided to fire Len Peterson for stealing.

Len had always been a difficult employee to manage, and my sixth sense told me there would be trouble.

I was right; Len filed a $1 million lawsuit proclaiming his innocence and charging the company with slander and character defamation. The trial lasted three months and ate up considerable time and company resources. It was extremely disruptive, not to mention the stress it caused me personally.

Fortunately, the incident was well-documented, and we eventually won the lawsuit. Although things did backfire a bit, it was certainly expected. Knowing Len, no one was really surprised. Although there was a lot of aggravation, the decision in final analysis was really worth it. Len was really the kind of person we didn't need around.

(*Note:* In a "controlling" culture, this kind of decision would likely have been made at the senior management level.)

Employee-Empowered Culture

The biggest risk I regret not taking was to accept the assignment in Chicago. I suppose hindsight is always twenty/twenty. At the time, the job seemed a bit of a stretch for me, since I had never had any field sales experience, and the idea of managing a major sales region, with no sales experience, seemed a little intimidating at the time. I have since tackled other management assignments in areas in which I had no fundamental technical grounding, and have done quite well. If I knew what I now know about how to successfully manage people, I would not have hesitated a second in accepting the Chicago assignment. The key to successful management is providing subordinates with strategic direction and vision as to where you want to be, and then counting on their technical skills and abilities to get you where you need to be going. This approach to management works very effectively for me.

22

INTERVIEW QUESTIONS— PERSISTENCE

KEY INTERVIEW QUESTIONS

There are many words that can be used to describe the trait of persistence, including resilience, strong staying power, determination, commitment, unyielding, dogged, stick-to-it-iveness, and dedication. Regardless of the words used to describe this trait, unless practiced to its extreme, it is a characteristic admired and sought after by most employers.

Here are some ways the employer might use the interview to examine your ability to be persistent:

- *Describe a work situation where you faced overwhelming odds but managed to prevail.*

  —What odds did you face?

  —Why was there resistance?

  — How and why did you prevail?

- *Tell me about a time when you knew you were right, but you were forced to abandon your position.*
  —*What was the issue?*
  —*What was your position?*
  —*What was the nature of the resistance?*
  —*How did you attempt to overcome this resistance?*
  —*What were the results?*
  —*What factors persuaded you to abandon your position?*
- *What can you tell me about your ability to be persistent?*
- *When you are championing an unpopular position, at what point are you prepared to abandon the cause?*
- *Which of the following terms is more descriptive of your style: persistent or accommodating? Why?*
- *Which term do you feel better describes you: well-liked or persistent? Why?*
- *Which term better describes you: persistent or flexible? Why?*
- *Tell me about a time when you had to convince others to support an unpopular cause. What did you do? What was the result?*

The quality of being persistent seems universally admired, as long as it is not carried to the extreme. People who are principled and willing to stand up for what they believe have long been the heroes of our culture. Individuals who have conviction and are willing to "hang in there" against the odds to eventually win, are what legends are made of. Thomas Edison, George Washington, Martin Luther King, Jackie Robinson, Churchill, Patton—the names go on and on. History rings with their names!

In industry, the term "persistent" can have both a positive and a negative meaning. On the positive side, it is used to describe people who are willing to "hang in there" in support of a just cause until they prevail. On the negative side, if one is seen as "too persistent," they might be

described as stubborn, argumentive, inflexible, unyielding, strong-willed, overbearing, hostile, aggressive, pesky,
and the like. Sometimes there is a fine line between being
loved and admired and being hated and detested. It's all a
matter of degree.

For the most part, organizations value individuals who
exhibit the positive side of the persistence equation. However, they may "run for the hills" if they feel you have a tendency to be overly persistent. So be careful which of these
two styles you describe when responding to interview questions about your level of persistence.

In the modern organizational climate, the "employee-
empowered" culture supports and encourages diverse
viewpoints. In this kind of environment, it is believed that
continuous improvement can only be brought about when
people challenge and change the traditional way of doing
things. At first, such viewpoints may not have popular
support and there may be resistance. But, eventually,
through positive persistence, the new idea may be tried
and, if effective, adopted as the new way of doing things.
Unless people are willing to be persistent and assertive
with respect to their views, the organization will cease to
grow and obsolescence will set in.

Today's organizational climate values the change agent,
the one who brings new ideas and positive change to the organization. Being an effective change agent requires persistence—the willingness to stand up for your values and
beliefs in the face of opposition. In this context, persistence
is seen as a valued trait sought in preferred employment
candidates.

INTERVIEW STRATEGY

When responding to interview questions used by employers
to determine your persistence, you will want to show that
you are willing to stand up for your beliefs and convictions,
and that you are willing to express your views openly despite initial resistance and lack of popularity. The message
received by the employer is that you are principled and have

strong convictions. It also communicates that you are assertive, and have sufficient self-respect and confidence to do what you believe to be right.

To demonstrate this trait in the interview, you will need to be prepared to describe occasions when you fought for your beliefs and were successful in convincing others to try your ideas. In citing such examples, you will want to share examples where the results were particularly favorable.

What you want to avoid, however, is sharing as an example of persistence behavior, those times when your persistence passed the line of reasonableness and turned into aggressive, confrontive, or outright hostile behavior. This is not the type of persistence that employers are seeking. There needs to be a tempering of this aggressive behavior in favor of a more flexible style that acknowledges the possible validity of contrary viewpoints.

When asked in the interview at what point you will back off on an issue you feel strongly about, an appropriate answer is "at the point when you sense that others are beginning to feel alienated by your persistence." In such cases, both parties need to be able to walk away with their personal dignity intact, and simply acknowledge the right of one another to disagree. Persistence beyond this point may win the battle but lose the war. Nothing is gained by either party when effective working relationships are ruptured by inflexible egos.

CLASSIC ANSWERS

Probably the time when I faced the greatest resistance was when I recommended we do away with traditional lines of progression and pay rates based on job level and move to a "pay-for-knowledge" based system. This initially met with considerable resistance, and I was told the union would never buy it.

So, I took the bull by the horns and formed a joint union/management continuous improvement team. One of our key objectives was to find ways to make jobs more interesting and stimulating. I introduced the idea of doing away with conventional job structure and providing employees more flexibility in what they do. I also introduced the idea of paying people for knowledge and results. The union loved the idea! Today we have a "high-performance work system" with pay tied to a combination of knowledge and results.

The outcome has been phenomenal! In five years, we have decreased the workforce 25 percent (with the union's blessing), and productivity has increased by nearly 20 percent.

* * *

Although I still feel it is a good idea, there was one time when I had to back off from an idea I strongly supported. I recommended that we initiate an exempt employee job posting system requiring that all professional and managerial job opportunities be posted openly for any employee who was interested to apply. After exploring the results realized by other employers using such a system and preparing detailed program recommendations for management approval, it became very clear that certain members of senior management simply would not support such a system.

I met with each dissenting senior manager individually to discuss their objections and to see what could be done to design around them. Although most admitted they were supportive of the general idea of job posting, it became apparent that they just did not want to have to deal with explaining their reasons for rejection when they turned people down. Feelings were so strong that it was evident support for the program was not going to be there. Since I'm not Don Quixote, I don't feel there's much future in jousting with windmills. I have since moved on to other things.

* * *

I am a combination of persistent and flexible. I think both terms describe me well. I hope you don't feel that I'm hedging the issue, but I honestly believe it's a toss-up. If I believe in something strongly, I can be extremely persistent in promoting my views. On the other hand, I am quite willing to listen to the points others make in support of the counterview.

For me, it's not a matter of ego. If someone else can present a compelling counterargument with points I haven't considered, I am quite willing to concede my position in favor of the opposing viewpoint. I have no problem doing that. On the other hand, I will insist that my viewpoint gets a fair and honest hearing. I won't easily yield my position unless someone is able to present a well-founded counterviewpoint, or point out some fallacy in current thinking.

I feel I am both persistent and, at the same time, flexible and open to new ideas and ways of thinking about things. We can all learn something from each other.

23

CLOSING THE INTERVIEW

It is surprising to me that in all of the books that I have seen on the topic of interviewing, I've seen very little on the subject of how to effectively close the interview. There are things the candidate can do during the close of the interview to considerably enhance the prospects of an employment offer. That is the subject matter of this chapter.

From the candidate standpoint, there are six key elements of an effective interview close. These are:

1. Expression of interest.
2. The value statement.
3. Requesting feedback.
4. Establishing the "path forward."
5. The "thank you."
6. The parting impression.

Since these are pretty much in the order in which they should occur during the interview closing, I will follow this same sequence in systematically discussing each of these critical, and often overlooked, elements of the employment interview.

EXPRESSION OF INTEREST

If you are interested in the job—tell them. I can't tell you how many times candidates who have a genuine interest in the job neglect to tell the employer this at the close of the interview discussion. I would estimate that this number could be 80 percent or better. What a shame!

Think about it for a moment. From the employer's standpoint, here we are at the end of the interview day. The candidate has spent a full eight hours with us, been interviewed by 12 people, had the job explained any number of ways, answered all his or her questions, explained our compensation policy, detailed our benefit coverages, discussed our performance evaluation system, and here we are at the close of the interview, and the candidate seems noncommittal. There is no expression of interest in the position so we really don't know one way or the other. Is he interested? Not interested? We just don't know. Exit candidate number one.

Enter candidate number two. Now this candidate is a real live wire. She has been full of questions all day long and seemed quite enthusiastic throughout a good deal of our discussion. Now we are at the close of the interview, and here is what she says:

I just want you to know how much I enjoyed the day and the effort everyone went through to answer all my questions and explain all the aspects of the job and the work environment here at the Tower Company. This has been quite an exciting day for me, and I want to let you know that I am very interested in the position described to me. This sounds like a very challenging and stimulating opportunity—exactly what I'm looking for. I know that I could do an excellent job for you, and hope that you are equally as excited with my candidacy. I would very much enjoy working here from everything I've heard today.

And now the sixty-four thousand dollar question, "Assuming relatively equal qualifications, which of these two candidates would you hire—candidate number one or candidate number two?" Could the answer be more obvious?!!

The lesson then is that if you are truly interested in the position for which you have just finished interviewing, tell them you are interested. Let them hear and see your enthusiasm for the job.

THE VALUE STATEMENT

Following statement of your interest in the position, you will want to add a value statement. This is simply a brief statement by you of one or two key ways the organization will benefit from bringing you aboard in the position. Here is a sample value statement:

Mary, I am really excited about this position and know I could do an excellent job for you. I already have some ideas for tackling the turnover problem, which I believe could quickly turn things around for you in that area. I think my experience with the development of variable compensation plans should also be an asset to your efforts to link executive compensation with company performance. The program we designed and installed at Newton Company has proven quite successful, and I know that top management is pleased with the results. I think I could do something comparable here.

Stating your confidence in your ability to make substantive contributions in key areas of concern to the employer is certainly going to heighten interest in your employment candidacy. The interview close presents the perfect opportunity to reinforce this impression by using an appropriately worded statement of value.

ASKING FOR FEEDBACK

This is another one of those areas that continues to surprise me, as candidates finish the interview day and neglect to ask for some basic feedback concerning the outcome of the interview. After a full day of questions and give-and-take between the parties, it is certainly not unreasonable to ask for some preliminary feedback on the status of your candidacy.

Here is an example of a way in which this could be done:

Dave, I want you to know that I really enjoyed the day, and that at this stage I am interested in the position of Accounting Manager. I was wondering if there is interest in me for this position as well. Can you provide me with some preliminary feedback on how things went from your standpoint?

This type of inquiry will almost always provide you with some feedback on your candidacy. It may or may not be exactly what you wanted to hear, but nothing ventured, nothing gained. Even if the answer is negative, it still might be an advantage to be aware of this fact at this stage of the process. This provides you with one last chance to remove the remaining objection before you depart for the journey back home.

I have personally seen cases where the candidate, upon getting negative feedback during the interview close, was able to completely turn the tables and regenerate interest in his or her candidacy.

If a candidate is going to be rejected, nine out of ten cases it will be for one of two primary reasons:

1. Lack of technical proficiency in a given area.
2. Lack of fit with the organization's culture.

Using some careful interview skills and some equally carefully worded questions, candidates are sometimes able to pretty much isolate the specific cause of the disinterest. In certain cases, the decision is based on the negative perception of one or two members of the interview team, who may not have a full understanding of the candidate's capabilities in the area in question.

Sometimes by citing contrary evidence to counter these perceptions, and by offering to provide the names of key references who are intimately familiar with your qualifications in this questionable area, you can turn the interview completely around and rekindle interest in your candidacy. Again, I have personally witnessed this phenomenon on more than one occasion. Although it may be a long shot, if you are really interested in the job, you may well want to give it a try.

On the other hand, if there is interest is in your employment candidacy, you will want to pay particular interest to the "degree" of that interest. This could provide some good clues as to how well leveraged you may be when it comes time for negotiations over the particulars of the job offer.

For example, if the employer says, *"I think at this point we have some initial interest, Jane, but I'll have to get back to you in a couple of days,"* you know one thing. However, if the interviewer states something to the effect, *"Jane, we are very excited about the idea of you joining us, and we plan to call you with an offer by tomorrow,"* this tells you something quite different. In the second instance, you are likely far more leveraged to negotiate your job offer than in the first example.

Be tuned-in to what the employer has to say about your candidacy, and note, in particular, the level or degree of interest in you. This will come in handy later when you are ready to discuss the particulars of your employment offer. Remember, the greater the employer's excitement and enthusiasm, the more leveraged you will be!

ESTABLISHING THE "PATH FORWARD"

It is a good idea during the interview close to request information concerning the next steps. When can you expect to hear from them? What does the employer see as the next steps and approximate timing?

It can be disconcerting to be interviewed and then not hear anything for several weeks. You are now in that awkward position of not knowing the outcome and are uncertain whether or when to place a follow-up call to the employer concerning your status. Or, perhaps, you should simply wait it out. If you call, you may appear to be pesky, but if you don't, they may simply forget about you. You are on the horns of a familiar dilemma.

In recent years, with the extent of corporate downsizing and numbers of well-qualified persons on the market, it seems that companies are becoming infamous for dragging out the employment decision. With the need to do much more with far fewer people, hiring managers are almost paranoid about making the right employment decision. Decision paralysis often sets in as the hiring manager, wanting to hire the best possible person, interviews candidate after candidate, not able to make that final decision. This will drag on for months on end if you let it.

As the employment candidate, the best way to manage this dilemma is to inquire about the "path forward" during the close of the interview discussion. Ask such questions as, *"John, where do we go from here? When can I expect to hear from you?"* In this way, you force some kind of commitment to follow up with you by a reasonable date.

If that date arrives, and you have not yet gotten the word, you now have a legitimate reason to call. Simply remind the hiring manger of their commitment to you. Here is an example of how this might be handled:

> *Sharon, this is Mike Jacobsen calling. From our discussion, I had expected to hear from you by last Friday concerning the outcome of my employment interview with Jordan Company. I thought perhaps I had somehow missed your call, so thought I would call and see where we stand. What's happening? Where are we at this point?*

This should serve to shake things loose one way or the other; at least you won't be sitting there for several more weeks wondering what is happening.

There is probably little to lose in making this kind of follow-up call. And, quite frankly, most employers will respect you for it. My years of experience in employment have shown that there is a direct correlation between length of time after the job interview and the probability of getting a "no interest" letter. The longer the time lapse since the interview, the higher is the probability that the answer that you will be getting is that there is no further interest in your employment candidacy. So, what do you have to lose in making this kind of follow-up call? Not a darn thing!

Because of the tendency for many employers to drag out the process, I often teach candidates a little trick to help them to force the issue. Remembering that with the lapse of time the chances increase that the employer will say "no interest," statistically speaking, you have very little to lose by doing this, but potentially a lot to gain. Here is the little trick.

Shortly after the appointed day on which the employer promised to get back to you but didn't, call and say something like the following:

> *Kevin, this is Barbara Dodson calling. I was expecting to hear something from you this past Friday concerning my employment candidacy, but since I didn't hear anything I thought I would give you a call instead.*
>
> *Kevin, although I continue to have an interest in the position at Watson Company, I needed to let you know that my circumstances have changed since we last talked. There are several things developing that will place me in a decision of needing to make some decisions shortly. So, I thought I would call you to see where we stand.*

If the employer has been dragging his or her feet, this should serve to get things moving quickly either one way or the other. If the employer is interested, they now know they can't continue to drag their feet, and that they need to get on with it. Failure to do so will increase the chance that they will lose you as a candidate. Further, the suggestion that you have some other things cooking will remind them of your value and heighten the sense of urgency to compete for your candidacy. In this case, you are liable to be getting an employment offer quickly.

Of course, it is a bit of a roll of the dice. The employer could just as soon make the decision to forgo your employment candidacy, in which event you have probably only accelerated the inevitable outcome. But at least you now know where you stand, and can get on with the rest of your job search. Sitting there, not knowing where you stand for weeks on end, can be a real negative drain psychologically.

SAY "THANK YOU"

Courtesy can go a long way in enhancing your image as someone who is polite and considerate. It's utterly amazing to me how many employment candidates have spent a full day in interviews where a lot of valuable time and energy was expended on their behalf, yet they fail to express any appreciation for the employer's efforts.

So, take time to be gracious and thank your host for the day. Here is a way this could be expressed:

George, I really appreciated the opportunity to be here today. Everyone was very cordial and helpful. I just wanted to say thank you for putting all of this together.

THE PARTING IMPRESSION

Well, now the interview is over, and its time to go home. But, there is one last thing to remember. You will want to leave a favorable parting impression. Just as you entered the interview with a firm handshake and a warm smile, you will want to leave the employer with that same positive impression.

Your friendliness and cordiality will be remembered and may just be that fine line between being the candidate they hire and being the one who goes away empty-handed.

INDEX